The Times of Our Lives

Our Lives

Tales from an Italian Neighborhood

I0152046

LOUISE RICCI MULGREW

ANTHOLOGY

ISBN 978-0-9983040-3-8

And I Owe It All to You...
To Jimmy B and my seven wonderful children,
my extended family, and the neighborhood
that inspired it all.

Foreword

Dear Reader,

The Times of Our Lives started out as a small plot concocted by me and my siblings to help our mom through a difficult time after our dad died. What started out as a blog evolved into three volumes of short stories and a monthly feature in the newspaper, *La Nostra Voce*, published by the The Italian Sons & Daughters of America. Mom's fun and engaging stories paint a romantic picture of growing up and raising a family in Cleveland, Ohio from the 1940s to the present.

Sharing her stories brought mom joy. Writing them down gave her a sense of purpose. Publishing them gave her confidence to try new things as she became passionately involved in the development of an award-winning short film, titled "In the Money."

Mom's to-do list was a long but unfinished one at the time of her death in 2020 from complications due to Covid-19. She may be gone, but the legacy of her love, laughter, and life lessons remains with us.

In honor of her memory, we her children: me, Patty, Jimmy, Michael, Margaret, Danny, Beth, and Donna, decided to finish the work she started by putting her stories all in one place. You'll meet us, as well as our father — her beloved husband Jimmy B — here in the pages of this book. We hope you enjoy reading it as much as she did writing it.

We will always be grateful to our parents for giving us the time of our lives.

Catherine Larose
August 2021

Contents

Contents (continued)

Contents *(continued)*

The Neighborhood

B ack in the day, before there were suburbs and exurbs, people grew up in neighborhoods, small villages in a way, ones bound by a shared culture, a common religion, and similar economic circumstances. I grew up in one such neighborhood, an Italian neighborhood, and raised my family there.

My grandchildren cannot imagine lives where they'd be able to walk to a local butcher, baker, or dry goods store. Nor can they imagine freely roaming the streets under the watchful eyes of all the "bella mamas," the mothers and grandmothers, who supervised dozens of children, most of them not their own.

"Be home when the streetlights come on," was a common cry kids heard as they pushed screen doors open after supper and bounded into warm, lightening bug-filled evenings.

My stories start way before the birth of my seven children. They start long before I was born in an Italian neighborhood in Cleveland. They start in the early 1900s with the immigration of boatloads of Italians from Southern Italy. They landed on Ellis Island or in New Orleans and spread out from there to set up tight-knit Italian neighborhoods like the one I grew up in.

We weren't alone in this migration, at least not in our little neighborhood. We had intrepid families who mixed and mingled with us. There were Germans, Romanians, and lots of Irish. We had one thing in common: we were all Catholic. Mixed marriages had more to do with marrying outside of your culture than your religion.

Back in 1959, mine was one of the few mixed marriages at the time. My husband was Irish. And my mother, always a practical woman, noted with approval that the combination made the most beautiful babies. Of course, she was slightly biased. But I'm getting ahead of myself.

Courtesy of Detroit Shoreway Community Development Organization.

The following stories became the inspiration for my blog, Bella Mama, and subsequently a series of books called, *The Times of Our Lives*. I used to tell my kids: "There are eight million stories in this neighborhood." I borrowed the line from the TV show *The Naked City* (1958–1963). And while I might not have eight million stories in this book, I hope you enjoy reading them as much as I did writing them. These are the stories of my own Bella Mama, Vincenza, and her three children, me (Louisa), my older brothers Carmen and Tony, and the neighborhood where it all happened.

The Black Widow Society

B ack in the day, my Grandmother Margherite, was a member of the informal social society I have come to call "The Black Widows." There's nothing more stereotypical than a widowed Italian woman wearing all black as a sign of her mourning and devotion. That was my grandmother's generation. That tradition, however, ended in 1960 when my father died unexpectedly at the far too young age of 47. I remember how eyebrows rose and tongues wagged when my mother, Vincenza, walked into the funeral parlor wearing navy blue.

After the funeral Mass, she leaned into the pew, stared down the pew and looked each Black Widow coolly in the eye. And she said, with the characteristic calmness that was her hallmark, "I was good to him when he was alive. I have nothing to prove now." From that day, and every day after, she continued to dress her way, despite stares and remarks. And, after that day, membership in the Black Widow Society saw a steady decline. Today, it is one tradition that is almost extinct.

And good riddance to it!

Bird on a Wire... or How To Make a Local Call

E very morning the Black Widows would attend 6:30 Mass at the local impromptu church, which was a hastily converted living room in a neighbor's house. The actual church, built by the "Vets" (returning veterans from the Second World War), was still another decade away.

Telephones were scarce, so the Black Widows' communication was conducted the old-fashioned way. In the summer, they stood in front of someone's house and called her name through the screen door. In the winter, they had to resort to walking up two or three steps and pound on the door, rosaries wrapped around their wrinkled knuckles.

Lena, our neighbor, and my Grandmother Margherite's best friend, would just open the window, stick her head out and yell across the backyard, her shrill voice seeming to rustle the leaves on the grapevines that formed an arbor between our two houses.

"Margherite! "Margherite! *Va Subito!*" (Go Quick!) God forbid they should be late for Mass!

It was my daily 6:25 a.m. wakeup call: way too early for a ten-year-old who was not a morning person!

From my bedroom window, I could see that grape arbor and Corvo, the old black crow who lived there. Corvo watched the comings and goings of the neighborhood with unblinking interest. He would turn its head left and then right on passersby as if he was watching a tennis match. Occasionally, Corvo would puff out its chest and call: "Caw! Caw!"

A perfectly ordinary bird... a perfectly ordinarily ordinary call. Or so I thought.

The time it took Lena to leave the window to gather her missal and rosary, pin her black lace headscarf to her white hair, sip the last of the espresso, and slip out the backdoor, was approximately five minutes. It was five minutes of blessed silence before she met my grandmother, and their conversation began in earnest as they walked out of the driveway and all the way up the street.

Corvo, concerned that my slow-moving grandmother, would also be late for Mass, added his own voice:

"Margherite! Margherite! *Va Subito!*"

It not only turns out that bird could talk; his words became my second wake-up call of the day!

I Heard It Through the Grapevine

In our neighborhood, there were four ways to get the news. (Believe it or not, TV didn't exist yet). There were the three city newspapers: *The Cleveland News, The Plain Dealer,* and *The Cleveland Press.* And then there was Carmelle.

Carmelle handled the "local news" of the neighborhood, everything from births, deaths, and all things in-between. The most serious and scandalous news was shared in the local Italian dialect, Coronese. Normal news was dispensed in broken English. And all news was punctuated with the appropriate hand gestures for which Italians are famous.

Carmelle would start her morning round of news gathering only after 6:30 Mass, much to the annoyance of the neighborhood widows who had to wait for her to arrive before serving cake and coffee in Grandma Margherite's kitchen. Unless it was summer! Then, conversations were held under the grape arbor in the backyard. Or, as my grandmother would say: "The back-a-yard."

For years, I always thought that the phrase "I heard it through the grapevine" originated with these early morning gossip sessions.

I remember one particular summer morning. Carmelle wasn't just late. She was *really* late. I could hear the women chatting outside my bedroom window. They all agreed that it must be a busy news day. Or, that something bad had happened. The latter was the most likely scenario in their superstitious minds.

My uncle, "Zi'Michele," (Uncle Mike), who happened to be passing through the "back-a-yard" on his way to work, took a more practical approach. He thought that Carmelle must have stumbled upon some juicy gossip and couldn't tear herself away. He decided to reassure the ladies. "Ma Dai... don't worry. If Carmelle died today, even Jesus couldn't find her."

Waking the Dead

I f you've ever lived in an old house, one built in the early 20th century, chances are that, at one time or another, it had a dead body in it. Not the kind of body you see on a television crime show, but a relative who had died at home.

Back in the day, funerals were held at home in peoples' living rooms. Funeral homes only came into widespread commercial use in the 1930s and 1940s, which was not in time for the recently deceased Beppo and his widow Bina.

Upon hearing the news, Carmelle and the Black Widows rapidly sprang into action: cooking, preparing a wreath for the door, and providing moral support to Bina. Once all the preparations were in place, they made the pilgrimage to Bina's house to pray the Rosary.

Now, it's normal to expect a certain amount of wailing along with tears and prayers. It's part of the culture. What wasn't normal was the sight of six Black Widows bursting through the front door, shrieking, and crossing themselves.

I was pitching pennies with my brothers against the side of our house when we saw this mad, mass exodus of the Widows and all the mourners. Our eyes grew wide in a combination of wonder and fright. You would have thought poor Beppo had risen from the dead which, in an Italian, Catholic, and superstitious neighborhood such as ours, was quite possible.

Just then Zi'Michele stepped outside and onto the top step of Bina's house.

"What happened? What happened?" we pressed him.

"You know Beppo. He could never sit still. Right in the middle of a Hail Mary, he sat straight up," Zi'Michele said.

"He rose from the dead?" Tony asked.

"No, *cidrule* (cucumber/stupid)!" Carmen said with the authority of an older brother. "He was never dead to begin with."

"Oh no, he's dead all right," said Zi'Michele, who was an expert on everything. He paused and took a long drag on his Camel cigarette. "His last meal was *pasta fazool* (*pasta fagioli*) and, apparently, he had a little gas."

The Heat is On... Not!

My grandchildren are not wrong when they say I come from another century. Growing up we didn't have cell phones or telephones. When it came to news, we had Carmelle. We didn't have refrigerators, we had ice boxes. Ice was delivered and installed on the side of the box. As the ice melted, the water would drip into a pan underneath the box. And we emptied it regularly.

We didn't have thermostatic heating either. We had a coal furnace. A truck came and delivered coal. The truck backed up and inserted a discharge chute into an opening in the side of the house. The opening was our coal chute and it emptied into the basement. As the coal tumbled down the chute it made a machine gun sound as it bounced off the metal walls: *rat-a-tat-tat-tat*...

A cloud of black dust would snake its way up the stairs and into the house. We were constantly wiping coal dust off our furniture and the dog, who always slept in front of the basement door.

Our job, mine, and my brothers, was to shovel the coal into the coal box. We also shoveled the coal into the furnace to heat the house. The house was always cold! The furnace was always hungry, and we couldn't shovel fast enough to feed it.

We emptied the ashes from the bottom of the furnace into another box. In winter, we scattered the ashes or cinders on the slippery sidewalks instead of rock salt, which was a luxury back then.

Although most people knew enough to empty the ashes from the furnace, no one seemed too concerned about cleaning the chimneys. This might have explained the sparks shooting from the chimney of the Bianchi house. The fire department made regular calls on our little street every winter. As for us kids, it was fascinating to watch.

As I explain it to my grandchildren, it seems like a lifetime ago. It *was* a lifetime ago. To quote my granddaughter, "Coal? It's positively Dickensian!"

A Package Deal

It used to be when you married into an Italian family you not only gained a husband, but you also gained a "live-in" mother-in-law. These women helped to cook, clean, and raise children, especially during the Second World War when fathers were away, and mothers had to work.

When my parents married back in the 1930s, my father's mother, Anna, came to live with us. We called her Nonnie, and she ruled the roost. Every morning, as my mother got ready for work at the local battery factory, she would cry as she left me and my two brothers in the capable, but cruel hands, of an aging widow who weighed 300 pounds if she weighed an ounce.

By the time we were old enough to drive Nonnie crazy, she was tired and cranky to say the least. We were no angels either. We would agitate her and run away knowing full well she could never catch us. When we were in our 'tween years, we would slide underneath the bed — just out of her reach — until the day she got her broom and made a clean sweep of, or swipe at, us. We laughed until we cried.

Nonnie was also capable of stealth attacks. She would sneak up on you while you were eating breakfast at the table and give you a *schiaf* (*schiaffo in testa*) or a smack to the head. Why? Just because.

The weapon of choice for all mothers-in-law in our neighborhood was the trusty rolling pin, which came in two sizes: short and long. I only saw Nonnie brandish it twice: the first time it was to chase a neighbor who had hit my Aunt Sophie. Nonnie broke out the big one and walked over to the neighbor's house to remind the woman that hitting someone was the domain of a family member and not a stranger.

"And don't you forget it!" she said. And then let loose with a string of some colorful curses in her native dialect.

The second time involved a stranger.

Coming home one day from the local grocers, we noticed the front door was open. When Nonnie did a quick tour of the house, she saw a stranger to the neighborhood, an inebriated woman, taking a nap on her pristine bed. Her sheets were her pride and joy: starched, embroidered and so white they were blinding.

Out came the rolling pin, and the only curse word she knew in her broken English. Luckily, my quick-thinking brothers woke the woman who, although disoriented, made a mad dash for the door while I tried to reason with Nonnie.

"Do you really want blood on those sheets?" I asked her.

Somewhat soothed, she paused long enough to think about it. And then she took the rolling pin and lovingly rolled out the wrinkles on her beautiful bed.

Chicken Run

A ll our food was fresh. There was no frozen food in plastic bags or microwavable containers. Food either came from the garden, or the large local ethnic market, called the Westside Market. The "processing" and cooking were done at home.

Every Saturday morning my mother took us to "The Market," as we called it. The streetcar (it cost only 3 cents) would be jam-packed with a representative of every family in the neighborhood. Good gossip and cooking tips were exchanged by all the grandmothers and mothers.

The Market had every kind of food imaginable; cultures converged there. There were German sausages, Polish pierogis, Greek pastries, and Hungarian chimney cakes. There were warm chestnuts in the winter, and all kinds of fruits and vegetables in summer. There were live animals: chickens, ducks, and rabbits, just to name a few.

My mother's shopping list always included a couple of live chickens for the week's dinners of chicken soup, Chicken Parmesan with pasta, roasted chicken breast, and chicken sandwiches. Occasionally we'd fish out chicken feet from a pot of pasta sauce and squirm. We'd skip dinner on those nights.

The butcher would wrap up the chickens in newspaper, and we'd carry them home by their feet, their heads upside down. You can imagine a streetcar full of immigrants each with two or three chickens firmly in hand. The squawking and the clucking — and that was from just the women — made for a very lively return trip. The entire streetcar emptied on the top of West 65th Street, and women and children made their way home.

To corral the chickens and not have them running loose in the house, we created a pen using four kitchen chairs. Inevitably one chicken always escaped and made a run for it. (And who could blame

A little closer to home...farm stands inside the Gordon Arcade.
Courtesy of Detroit Shoreway Community Development Organization.

her?) My brother Tony oversaw the chasing and catching of the poor things for "processing." We all ended up preferring meatballs to anything made with chicken. (After all, we never met any cows.)

Still, my mother was not above sending us to school with the biggest chicken sandwiches imaginable, lovingly wrapped in newspaper. It wasn't the chicken that made the sandwiches so big. It was the bread.

Growing up, we never had sliced bread: that was an American thing. As Italians, we purchased loaves of country-style bread from the local baker. And we cut them ourselves. The two slices my mother carved for each sandwich could have served the multitudes in the gospel story of the loaves and the fishes. We could have fed the whole school with the amount of bread she used.

If it wasn't chicken sandwiches, it was eggplant or fried pepper sandwiches. I used to beg my mother for bologna sandwiches and American bread. But, according to my mother, Oscar Mayer was for Germans, and American sliced bread would shame the baker.

Of course, such large slices of bread made it nearly impossible to fit into the toaster. We ended up toasting it in the oven which made the bread harder than Carrara marble. Thank goodness for coffee; we used it to dunk the bread and soften it.

Life was good — and flavorful.

It's a Small World

Everything we ever needed could be found within a boundary of two or three streets. As kids, we never felt the need to venture very far from home. The hot pavement was our playground. We pitched pennies against the curb and played kick the can in the middle of the street, all the while dodging semi-tractor trailers on their way to the air reduction factory at the bottom of the street.

In our pre-teens, we became more adventurous. Rumor had it there was an actual playground about four or five streets away located in what was then a predominantly Romanian neighborhood. Shoring up our courage, and in open defiance of our grandmothers' golden rule of "Don't leave the street!" we ventured out.

It was a whole new world. There we discovered kids who were not Italian! For years, we had thought the world was inhabited by only Italians. Imagine believing the world was that small? We met Irish, Romanian, and American kids. American kids meaning the third or fourth generation of any ethnic American who ate sliced white bread and bologna sandwiches.

The playground itself was a wonderland with a large baseball diamond populated by older boys. There were swing sets, monkey bars, and sliding boards that were at least nine or ten feet tall.

Not only did we continue to venture outside of our neighborhood because of that playground, but we also broke the "be home before the streetlights come on" rule. More than a few boys, my brothers included, ended up with "loose brains" because when their grandmothers caught them coming home late, they gave them each a whack to the head and a warning, "Don't you ever make me worry like that again."

Still, we were growing up fast and even the threat of violence didn't stop us. We continued to go to the playground and mix and mingle with our new friends. These were friendships that would last our entire lives. Eventually some of us even married some of these non-Italians. But that's another story for another time.

Who knew all those years ago what would happen? Where would life take us? What roads would we travel? How would we turn out? Who would become doctors, lawyers, police, or politicians? All we knew for sure is that we would stay friends forever, and we did.

*

Games People Play

n our neighborhood, everyone played games. There were sporting
competitions, like bocce and baseball; games of skill, like kick the
can, pitching pennies and marbles and, finally, games of chance.

I was already familiar with some of the games. Other games I came
to learn about through observation. Take dice for example. For the
longest time, I thought my father and his friends were throwing rocks
against a wall. I guess I was too busy to notice that these rocks had
spots on them. Not to mention, when I slowed down long enough to
look, a lot of money was also changing hands, and it wasn't pennies!

This game was called "craps." And it was taken very seriously. The
players came from all over, from other neighborhoods. It was that
popular. Later, I learned that some of those players were bookies,
loan sharks, card sharks, and professional gamblers of every stripe.
The men took care to keep the kids out of the way and occupied
while they played.

They arranged for diversions, and with those diversions, the
street took on the atmosphere of a carnival. Neighbors would sit outside on the benches in front of their homes and play music. There
were guitars, mandolins, and accordions. The music was beautiful
and the songs nostalgic. My favorite song was "Chitarra Romana."

Red wine, fresh lemonade, and espresso flowed in abundance.
Old men played morra, the Italian version of rock/paper/scissors.
On very hot nights, Zi'Michele (Uncle Mike) would open a fire hydrant, and we'd ran through the gushing stream of water until night
fell or we got tired.

Exhausted, we'd crawl into the nearest bed, and sometimes it
wasn't necessarily our own. We often stayed overnight at friends'
houses and woke up in the morning to the exact same breakfast ev-

eryone else had. One time, while eating my breakfast at my cousin Norma's house, I saw my Uncle Carmen reading a strange newspaper.

It turns out the newspaper was the racing form. When I asked him why he needed a racing form he told me it came in handy for learning math. In it you learned about odds, ratios, and fractions. And if you understood the math, you could pick a winner at the racetrack.

My two older brothers "studied" the racing form regularly. And as part of my education, they would often take me to the racetrack for a lesson in handicapping to see how numbers "work."

Carmen, who was always more frugal with his money, had $5.00 but was only going to bet $2.00. Tony, on the other hand, was going to put everything he had on "the nose of a filly." He had a hot tip. Somehow, he convinced Carmen to give him all his money. They bet the lot, and the horse finished so far back it ended up in the next race.

The only lesson I learned that day was not to let Tony talk me into anything.

Seventh-Inning Stretch

I n addition to the games we played on the street, we also attended professional games. We were a baseball neighborhood. And we were die-hard Cleveland Indians fans. (We also rooted for the Yankees but that's only because Joe DiMaggio played for them.)

When the Yankees came to Cleveland to play it wasn't unusual to see Joe DiMaggio down at the playground, hitting home runs out of the park and into the parking lot of a nearby factory. The boys would sit on the top of the backstop and cheer him on until they ran out of baseballs and Joe headed downtown to play at Municipal Stadium.

It was a well-known fact that Salvatore "Balls" Ballatore was the Indians' number one fan. If Sal weren't at home, he could be found at the ballpark rooting for his beloved Indians. Little did we know the Indians weren't the only thing he loved.

His wife, Gina, got used to his frequent absences. In fact, it suited her; it gave her time to enjoy the company of her friends.

One day, in August, Sal was late getting home from an afternoon game. The evening went by, and still no Sal. Neighbors just shrugged it off and figured he stopped in at a local bar and fell asleep.

One day turned into two, which turned into a week, and then a month and even a police investigation. And still no sign of Sal. Years went by, nine years in fact, when one day, Sal turns up on Gina's doorstep.

Gina, to say the least, was shocked. Once she could recover her voice, she asked him, "Ma, Sal what happened to you?!"

"Well you see there was this seventh-inning stretch..."

"A seventh-inning stretch for nine years?! It took you nine years to come home?"

Salvatore hung his head in shame. "I guess I lost count."

"Here, let me help you count," Gina said. "One, two, three strikes. You're out!"

The Gambler's Guide to Gaming

As children, we were never quite sure what our father did for a living. One day in first grade, at Waterson School, the teacher gave us an assignment: find out what our parents did for a living. Well, I certainly knew what my mom did. Like most neighborhood parents, she made batteries at the local Union Carbide factory. My father, because he was in and out of our lives, was another story.

When I asked my mom, she simply replied. "A lieutenant." I wasn't sure what that was, but it sounded important.

Satisfied, I returned to school the next day and told the class what my mom and dad did.

The teacher beamed, "Oh, your dad is in the army."

I put up my hand to protest but quickly took it down because I thought it might be poor form to correct the teacher. If dad was a lieutenant, I was pretty sure he wasn't in the army because I never saw him in uniform. But then again, what could possibly explain his extended absences?

A few years later, when a pool table showed up in our living room, along with my father, a better profession came to mine — a pit boss. Every weekend, from seven till eleven, we were sent to my grandmother's house. What we didn't know was that the pool table had been converted into a craps table and our living room was now a gambling den!

A few years later, I learned that in addition to being a construction foreman, my father's true calling was as a professional gambler. One of the few pieces of advice he gave me in my youth was, "Never play with scared money," or never play if you are nervous about losing. The dice or cards always know.

As you make your way through this book, you will find that a bit of the gambling gene has rubbed off on all my family. My brothers Carmen and Tony were experts at cards, dice, and horses. My husband Jimmy also handicapped us out of more tight financial spots than I care to remember.

As for me, craps was always my game. I liked the odds. And there was something almost musical about it. The noise those black and white cubes made as they rolled down the table. Call them the tumbling dice. My children smile when I describe it that way. They are also avid students of the game, many games for that matter.

One day, when I discovered my youngest son running a casino in our garage, I had to feign shock and dismay. I mean, what would the other parents think? And then there was the Saturday afternoon games of Night Baseball with their father, where pennies were won and lost — mostly lost — to the "house." In those days, I was "the bank."

And as the bank, I gave my children the following advice, "Of all strategies, knowing when to quit may be the best." To which their father added, "And never bet against the house," as he proceeded to collect their lost bets from the kitchen table.

A-Tisket, A-Tasket

When I was a teenager, the highlight of my summer was the annual picnic held at the county fairgrounds.

The "nonne," i.e., grandmas, spent three days preparing the food. They made loaves of fresh bread, which they thickly sliced and filled with all kinds of Italian lunch meats: capicola, lardo, mortadella, salami, and prosciutto.

There were all kinds of pastas made with "secret sauces" that the nonne jealously guarded. They were passed onto the next generation only on deathbeds, and if you weren't quick enough... goodbye secret recipe!

For dessert, there was freshly cut watermelon and anginetti cookies. These cookies are soft, not too sweet, and look like little knots. They have the most intense lemon-flavored icing and are delicious with coffee. For drinks, there was wine for the adults and lemonade for the kids.

You could hear all the grandmas singing as they went about their catering duties. They enlisted the help of their daughters who had the day off from the factory because it was Saturday.

Most fathers took advantage of their wives and kids being away to make a run to the racetrack. And this was good because it left the teenage boys in charge. I will tell you more about that later.

Large hampers were packed with ice and food and set on the kitchen table ready to be carted to the waiting bus.

Since the arrival of the bus was taking a little longer than planned, all the women sat outside on the front stoop gossiping, my grandmother and mother included. When the bus arrived, my brothers, Tony and Carmen, and I ran up to the women to hurry them along.

And hurry they did. They grabbed their hats and fans and followed the excited teenagers to the waiting bus. And off we went.

We sang all the way to the fairgrounds. Our favorite song was the picnic song, or what is more commonly known as Ella Fitzgerald's "A-Tisket, A-Tasket."

Little did we know that this song proved to be quite prophetic. As we arrived at the picnic table, we realized that we'd forgotten our basket on the kitchen table in our rush to the bus.

We weren't worried though. Being an Italian picnic, there was plenty of food to go around. In fact, there was enough there to feed half the city. For years we thought Jesus must have been Italian because he was so good at feeding people all those loaves and fishes!

The Bus Stops Here

I often wonder what puts people on their paths in life. Some people find themselves on yachts, some in suburban houses, some in the ghetto, and one or two in jail. How did they get there?

In the case of my two brothers, what took them to a short stint in jail was a picnic bus. That's right — that bus — the one that took us to our annual summer picnics. But who could have predicted that? Certainly not my grandmother, who was the actual instigator of the "crime." I guess you could blame my brothers' flawed logic or my mother's not-quite-legal explanation. But more on that a bit later.

One summer, the morning of our annual picnic, the rented bus broke down. Everyone was disappointed. My grandmother pulled my two brothers aside and told them to go and see about getting another bus.

So off Tony and Carmen went to the bus company. When they arrived, they found only one bus was left, a brand new one that cost an additional $50.00 to rent. There was no negotiating with the manager; he refused to budge. It was mid-day Saturday and closing time, so he dismissed the boys with a jerk of his head and a "Get outta here! And don't come back until you have some money."

Not wanting to disappoint their grandmother, and calling upon their well-honed skills with cars, they jump-started the bus and drove it to the schoolyard. In their minds, they thought they could borrow it for a few hours and have it back in the parking lot before anyone knew it was gone.

Naturally, everyone was impressed when they rolled into the parking lot in a brand-new bus. My grandmother was so proud, and my mother was astonished. So off we all went.

A few hours later, the local police showed up at the fairgrounds looking for the "bus drivers." They had an appointment with the judge, and jail!

My grandmother, who was sure this was all a mistake, explained patiently to the officer in her broken English, "Ma, No! No steal. Change the bus. They good boys!"

"No ma'am, they took it."

My mother stepped in, "But we thought it was an even exchange with the broken bus."

"That's not how the owner sees it."

So off we all went down to the courthouse, with my brothers in handcuffs and a collection of loose change from the neighbors to help spring the boys from jail.

And that's how they ended up in jail. I guess you could say, *the bus stops here*, I told my mother when we arrived at the courthouse. She was not amused.

That little episode didn't alter my mother's steadfast love and support for my brothers one iota. In fact, she was a rock of love and solidarity. Qualities all mothers possess.

Everyday Miracles

There's an expression: "miracles happen every day if you just know where to look." Growing up on our street, miracles were a common occurrence. Sometimes there was divine intervention and, other times, everyday people were at the right place at the right time. And then there were things that remain unexplained till this day.

Take the annual procession on the feast of Our Lady of Mount Carmel. It always happened on a Sunday afternoon at 3:00 p.m. Since the feast occurred in mid-July, the odds were always in our favor when it came to the weather. It was always a sunny Sunday afternoon, except for one Sunday when it poured nonstop all morning and afternoon, until 2:55 p.m.

The Supreme Knight of the Knights of Columbus conferred with the parish pastor, Father Cesare, about cancelling the procession due to weather. It would have been a first in the history of the church. Father Cesare shook his head, glanced at the sky, and simply said, "No."

As Father Cesare stepped outside of church with the faithful behind him, the clouds parted, the sun appeared, and the sidewalks dried instantly. The procession went forward as scheduled.

Then there's the story of my brothers, Tony and Carmen, who were at Edgewater Park playing on top of a picnic table. They were jumping from tabletop to tabletop, something they really shouldn't have been doing. Tony looked up and out over Lake Erie and noticed a small boy struggling in the water. The little boy was in over his head. Tony and Carmen jumped down from the table, ran to the beach, and dove in the water. Tony was the faster swimmer and reached the boy just in time to pull him to shore. They were in the right place at the right time.

Courtesy of Detroit Shoreway Community Development Organization.

We were a neighborhood of great faith. I always tell my children, "Have faith in God who has faith in you." It was faith that enabled my favorite cousin, Norma, to walk after being stricken with polio. I was sure that if I lit every candle in church and prayed hard, she would walk again. And she did. And while Father Cesare commended my great faith, he also expressed his grave concern regarding my pyrotechnic message to God which nearly burned down the church.

In addition to miracles, there were also signs. One day, a cross appeared on the front door of the corner bar. Sun, rain, clouds, it didn't matter. Everyday a cross appeared on the door. That didn't stop anyone from frequenting the bar. That was, in fact, seen as a sign of approval.

Just out of curiosity, we asked Fr. Cesare his opinion as to why a cross would appear on the bar door. He just shrugged his shoulders and said, "If our Lord could turn water into wine, why shouldn't we enjoy it." *A Salut!*

Sock Hops, Soda Shops, and Sororities

I t you're familiar with the 1970s TV show, *Happy Days*, you'll know that they do a pretty good job of capturing my teen years.

Our high school, West High School, reminded me of Pemberley, Mr. Darcy's mansion in the novel *Pride and Prejudice*. It was a grand building. There were four floors, and there were two sets of stairs. The right side went upstairs while left side was for downstairs traffic. But what went on inside those stately walls was more like *Grease* than *Northanger Abbey*.

Once a week we would have a dance, called a "canteen" in the gym. We set up a record player, and someone would spin the latest 45s. We danced the jitterbug, the stroll, and the bop. Some of the kids were so good they went on to dance on *American Bandstand*. And although the popular TV show originated in Philadelphia, the phrase Rock 'n Roll was born in Cleveland.

At the end of the year, the schoolyard became a midway with rides and games. Groups of girls, dressed in their sorority or club colors, strolled the grounds, flirting with bad boys but making dates with good boys. Girls belonged to clubs called sororities. My sorority was called Zeta Chi. Our jackets were black and white, and we ruled the school. Oh yes, and I almost forgot (my grandchildren are also reading this), we also went to class!

𝄢

Girls' Night Out...
Well, Almost

Growing up as the only girl in my neighborhood was bad enough — the boys treated me like one of the guys — but having two older brothers who were overprotective was worse. It was impossible for me to get a date in my neighborhood.

The boys would hang out on the street corner at night. They were usually dressed in cuffed blue jeans and white T-shirts with a pack of Lucky Strikes rolled up in the sleeves. And here they would harmonize some doo-wop tunes. They were so good; they could have turned professional. They'd sing and watch all the girls go by. All except this girl. No sooner did I make it to the corner then my brothers intercepted me and escorted me back down the street.

But that didn't stop me from venturing forth into the other neighborhoods that bordered the playground. Here I met lots of nice boys who didn't know who my brothers were; they just knew they were dating an Italian girl. But just to play it safe, they always dropped me off a couple of blocks away from my street.

It wasn't long before Tony and Carmen and half the neighborhood left for the service (Armed Forces). Tony joined the Navy and Carmen joined the Air Force. This left an extra car at home for me: a black Cadillac.

The boys hadn't been gone long when I decided to test my newfound freedom and piled all my girlfriends into the Caddy and drove to the Band Box, an off-limits establishment for me according to my brothers.

I had wanted to go to the Band Box for years but being my brothers' hangout, I never dared. Once they were gone there was nothing to stop me. I was so excited. I got all dolled up in my best dress and high heels.

The parking lot was full when we pulled in and you could feel the energy in the air. I ushered my girlfriends through the door like a pro, like I had been a regular all these years. They were impressed and so was I if I do say so myself.

As soon as we crossed the threshold I caught sight of a familiar face sitting at the first table: it was Tony. He was on leave and had stopped at the Band Box for a drink before heading home.

It was a surprise. I looked at him and he looked at me. And then I just turned around at walked out the door like a pro.

The Dago Bombers

B elieve or not, there was a time when you could leave your doors open and your bicycle outside without fear of anything being stolen.

There were several reasons for this. First, the neighborhood Black Widows always kept a sharp eye out for people's comings and goings. Second, everyone knew everyone else and trusted them. Third, we were a poor neighborhood of immigrants so there wasn't anything to steal. People were into sharing.

As such, we took pleasure in the simple things in life. The Calabrese Hall on 69th Street hosted many a wedding or a dance. The Gordon Arcade, a favorite neighborhood hangout, had a roller rink and a cinema.

Our preferred place to eat was Arnold's Diner on the corner of 65th and Detroit. Sound familiar? That's right, just like the one in *Happy Days*. Only we had it first.

Members of the Vets Club (Veterans of Foreign Wars) were busy planning fundraisers for the new school as well as donating the hard labor to build it.

In the 1950s, a local group of guys created the Dago Bombers. They become known as a neighborhood gang. Back in the day, every neighborhood had its own gang, but they weren't like gang members in *Westside Story* or even worse, like today's gangs. They were more like the "Our Gang" of *The Little Rascals* fame. They were a band of brothers dedicated to keeping watch over the neighborhood and each other. One of the local guys, an artist by trade, crafted a Dago Bombers badge members wore with pride.

The Bombers were the epitome of cool with their leather jackets, cuffed blue jeans, t-shirts with packs of Lucky Strikes rolled up in their sleeves, sunglasses, and Brylcream slicked hair swept into ducktails or D.A.s as they were called. If you didn't know them, you'd cross the street just to avoid them.

I may joke about the Our Gang reference but make no mistake. They could be tough guys when they had to be. And that's really what made the neighborhood safe.

🙿

How I Met Your Father

Today's children ask for candy, sugary cereals, toys, and/or video games. However, my children never did. That's due in large part to the times. It was the 1960s, and because we didn't have a lot of extra money, they were happy with very little. What they did ask for, and couldn't get enough of, were my stories.

"Tell me a story!" They'd shout after dinner every night. And so, that's what I did.

One of their favorite questions was, "Where did I come from?" I just took a page from the 1960s mothers' handbook, and answered, "You came from the cabbage patch." Or, "You were delivered by the stork." Or, "you came in a basket that floated up onto the beach at Edgewater." But their favorite story was how I met their father.

I'd start by saying that Jimmy (their dad) was my brother Tony's friend. That was one strike against him. And my children would giggle as I counted off his defects on my fingers.

He was also Irish. That was strike two. My children knew they were half-Irish, but growing up in Italian neighborhood, that "side" of their heritage was a foreign concept to them.

And finally, he was kinda, sorta cute. But he wasn't one of the dark Italian boys that I was used to and preferred. He had blue eyes, brown hair, and pale skin. Strike three!

On the other hand, I thought he was perfect for my best friend Kay, who also happened to be Irish. But Kay had the good sense to have a crush on my darkly handsome cousin, Wicky. So that was the end of that.

One day, I walked into the living room to find Jimmy sitting on our couch. I took one look at him, turned on my heel and walked out. Not my type. A few days later he was back, on the pretext of looking for my brother but he was there to ask me out.

Kay bet me a dollar that if I went out on a date with him, I wouldn't last five minutes. And as I am a gambling girl, I took that bet. That was going to be the best dollar I ever made, or so I thought.

Jimmy asked me to go to the "show" downtown. The show is what you now call the movies. I looked at my brother who just shrugged. Good, I thought, Tony wasn't going to kill him. And I accepted his offer. I smiled at Kay.

We went to see *Blackboard Jungle*. It was a group date. I figured if this guy turned out to be a dud, I could at least talk to some friends.

The movie barely got started when some kid jumped on stage and started dancing to "Rock Around the Clock." People were yelling for him to get off the stage, and before you knew it the lights came up, they stopped the show, and we left. From there we went out to Diney's Diner for cokes. It turned out that I kinda liked this guy. It was the most exciting, and expensive, first date I ever had. After all, it cost me a dollar.

๑

The White Box

Growing up I had two grandmothers. My grandmother Nonnie lived with us. My other grandmother, Margherite (Mamae), lived next door with my Aunt Mary.

After my Aunt got married and moved out, Mamae was left all alone. Mamae was busy enough during the day, but she was getting older, and my mom thought it would be a good idea if I went over there and spent the nights with her.

As a busy fifteen-year-old who was out with her girlfriends most evenings, my poor grandmother would wait up for me to come home before retiring for the night.

She didn't do it out of concern for my welfare, nor was she afraid to go to sleep on her own. The neighborhood couldn't be safer what with everyone sitting out on their porches. And strangers never ventured onto our streets as the unofficial neighborhood gang or guardians, the Dago Bombers, were always there to keep watch.

No, my grandmother would wait up for me out of ritual and superstition. Every night she reenacted the same routine.

"Louisa!" she would call to me when she heard me come home. "*Vieni qua*/Come here." (All of this was done in her Southern Italian dialect.)

And then she'd ask me to take a white box out from under her bed. After I gave her the long white box, she laid it lovingly on the bed and then lifted the lid. She opened the white tissue paper and carefully removed the contents.

"*M'uarda*, (but look) *E cosi bella*' (it's so beautiful)," she would say as she held up and admired a new girdle with attached garters. Next, she laid out her new, white, and never worn Playtex bra; the cotton was so stiff it practically stood at attention. Then she pulled out a pair of silk stockings, followed by her most beautiful dress, a hat, and a string of pearls. The entire process took twenty minutes!

She looked at me expectantly as I dutifully admired her treasure. And then she looked me in the eyes and say, "Remember, you take this box to the funeral home when I die. Do you promise?"

The first time she said it I was appalled by the thought. In my young mind, there was something rather ghoulish about it. By the fourth or fifth night, I had gotten used to the idea.

After about a week, I asked her why she took out the box and its contents every night.

Her answer was, "I take them out to show God, because I want him to recognize me when he calls me home."

I couldn't argue with that logic, but I was getting tired of spending all that time every night making sure God recognized my grandmother.

After about ten days, I convinced her to leave the box under the bed.

To accomplish this, I asked her, "It's God, right? I'm sure he has a good memory. He sees *tutte le cose belle in quella scatola. Lo vede ogni notte.*" She had to agree with that logic God did indeed see these beautiful clothes every night.

She was a little leery at first, but I also told her it was for the good of the fabric. After all, she didn't want to arrive in front of St. Peter all wrinkled, right? She seemed satisfied with that. I thought of all my unconfessed sins and God's long memory and made a mental note to go to confession.

It wasn't long before her health started to fail, and her daughters thought it best to move her in with my Aunt Rosie. A couple of years later my grandmother had died. The day she had been preparing for had finally arrived. I went to the funeral home expecting to see her laid out in all her finery. You can imagine my shock and dismay when I saw she was dressed in an outfit I didn't recognize and I'm sure she didn't pick.

When I asked my Aunt Rosie what had happened to the white box, she looked at me with a strange look on her face.

"What white box?" she asked.

"The box that was under her bed," I said.

"I never saw any box," my Aunt Rosie said, truly puzzled.

My Aunt Mary, my mother, and I all looked at each other. We knew the importance of that box.

I could read the concern on their faces and see their thoughts battling with their logic. It was after all a silly, superstitious question in this modern age in the new world.

"How was God going to recognize their mother?"

I looked at her lying peacefully in her own white box and I said to my mother and my aunts.

"*M'uarda* (but look) *Come e bell' lei* (how beautiful she is). Who could forget that face? Certainly not God."

They had to agree!

✍

Lack of Education

There are some movie phrases that over the years have become iconic.

"Here's looking at you, kid." — *Casablanca*

"What we have here is a failure to communicate." — *Cool Hand Luke*

"I'll be back." — *The Terminator*

"Lack of Education" was a phrase coined by my husband Jimmy. It seemed to be a catch all for bad behavior or lack of manners or both. He first used it in high school as a dig against his two older brothers who had quite a reputation at West High School.

His oldest brother Frank knew everybody. He was a joker and wherever he went laughter often followed but mostly at the expense of overly strict teachers. He was the glue in afternoon detention sessions holding together a diverse group of students.

John, the middle brother, was always there to back Frank up and so, naturally, they were well known to teachers and students. Teachers dreaded them, fellow students wanted to be like them, and trouble was their best friend.

One teacher was once heard to ask John if there were any other brothers due to attend high school. Johnny was pleased to announce that West High could look forward to a third brother, Jimmy, the next year. The teacher heaved a heavy sigh and was heard to say, "Oh no, not another one."

My husband was also a bit of an instigator and so you can imagine the havoc he caused in high school, especially with his brothers there. With his angelic face and the charm of a natural born sales-

The Wild Colonial Boys – Johnny, Jimmy, Simon and Frank

man, Jimmy usually managed to dodge the wrath of his teachers, leaving Frank and John to bear the brunt of the blame.

And then with all innocence and conviction, he'd deliver the bad news to his father Simon, a tough old Irishman if ever there was one. Frank and John were in trouble again. Simon would peer over the obituary section of the *Cleveland News* and scowl. Jimmy, was only too pleased to venture his explanation as to the bad behavior of his two brothers, "Lack of education, Pa. Lack of education."

Concerned for their younger brother's welfare, Jimmy was quickly racking up as many detentions as Frank. Or perhaps because he was cramping their style, the older brothers decided it would be best if Jimmy attended Catholic school. And so, the brothers pooled their resources and packed him off to St. Edward High School with the warning he'd better graduate or else. Jimmy graduated the Class of '55, as he was fond of saying, but not before serving his fair share of detentions by digging the new school's foundation.

Frank and John joined the service (Armed Forces) and when they came out, they went on to become, respectively, a policeman and a lumberyard foreman. They were both as popular out of high school as they were when they were in it. People knew and loved them. And they never stopped looking after their little brother.

I suspect that when Jimmy went before St. Peter at the pearly gates, his two brothers were there to meet him, and as St. Peter looked down the long list of Jimmy's life, noting all his detentions, I can just hear Franky and Johnny whispering into the gatekeeper's ear. "Lack of education, Peter. Lack of education."

❧

Mr. Sandbag

S andbagging: *when a player in a game chooses not to play their best just to hustle you. They hide their talent or skill until they're ready to win the game or seal the deal, usually scooping up your money at the same time.*

In our family, a sandbagger was also someone who "hid" their true winnings or kept some extra cash in their pockets. Take my brothers for example. Carmen was a great sandbagger. He always had money. And Tony was always broke. When Tony needed a "loan" he naturally went to Carmen.

Carmen, who had a soft heart, was also a soft touch. Tony always knew he could count on him. Their conversation would usually go something like this:

"Hey Carmen, you got any dough?"

"No," Carmen would answer. Carmen, being the sensible one, not only had money in his pocket but he also had savings.

"Ah, c'mon, you gotta have something. Today is payday. I got a hot tip on a horse."

Carmen just shook his head. I already knew where this conversation was heading because I had seen my brothers in action before. Tony would always promise to double Carmen's money, and Carmen would always hand over his money in the hopes of bettering his investment. In time, Carmen learned to hold back (sandbag) and tell Tony that he only had limited funds in his pocket. He'd say he had five dollars when he really had ten. I knew that, but Tony didn't.

Round about this time there was a popular song called "Mr. Sandman." It was a very catchy tune and, with one slight change, I used to walk around the house and serenade my brother Carmen. But instead of singing Mr. Sandman, I'd sing Mr. Sandbag. Boy, did he ever get mad. It wasn't because he felt I was insulting him; no, he was afraid I would blow his cover.

According to Tony, the opportunities to make money were everywhere. First there was the racetrack. Then there was Johnny "Spots" Moretti's house. Johnny "Spots" had a pool table in his living room that was quickly and easily converted into a craps table on Friday nights. As luck would have it, and it's always luck, Tony was able to convert those spots into cash. He made enough cash to fund a trip to Las Vegas for himself, Carmen, and their favorite cousin, Dickie Vee.

Back in those days, a day trip to Vegas was quick and cheap and you could always count on hotels to comp the high rollers. If you looked closely, my high-rolling brother Tony would have a fifty-dollar bill wrapped around fifty singles. Mr. Big Spender. And spend he did.

As expected, he burned through his cash, Dickie Vee's cash, and Carmen's cash in less than six hours. They had another ten hours to kill and they were flat broke. Tony was dejected, Dickie Vee was disappointed, and Carmen was relieved that Tony believed he was also broke. But no, unbeknownst to Tony, Mr. Sandbag still had twenty dollars in his pocket. That money was intended to buy them a nice dinner and drinks prior to taking off for home.

In the hotel room, Tony lay across the bed flipping cards into an empty bowl. Dickie Vee did a crossword puzzle, and Carmen watched the television to kill time. The minutes crawled by. Boredom hung like a wet blanket over the little group. Just an hour earlier they had been caught up in the sights and sounds of a casino and now they were cooling their heels in a hotel room.

Carmen glanced at his younger brother. He had never seen him look so forlorn. Before he knew it, his soft heart got the better of his hard head. He turned to Tony and said, "Mind if I play?"

Tony just shrugged and handed him the deck of playing cards.

"No need," Carmen said. "I have my own."

And with those words he pitched two crisp ten dollar bills into the bowl.

Tony and Dickie Vee jumped to their feet.

Tony hugged Carmen, "I knew you'd come through. I knew you'd take care of me. You always do!"

Carmen would protest, "This is it. This is absolutely the last time. No more."

But everyone knew that Carmen would always be there for Tony no matter what. No sandbagging there!

I Just Called
to Say...

S everal years ago, my favorite uncle, Danny, was in a bit of a jackpot. Not the kind where you win money. That's the dictionary
definition. Danny's jackpot was the opposite. The slang definition means you're in a bad spot.

Apparently, he had miscalculated on a few horse races and found
himself short of cash, and he didn't have the heart to tell his wife, my
Aunt Rosie. He thought it best to keep it quiet and not upset her. He
opted for a payday loan from Etna instead.

It was a good solution except that to get the loan he needed a
cosigner. And so, he asked my mother Vicenza. Mom had no problem cosigning but she swore Danny to secrecy. No sense having
Rosie mad at them both. My mother knew that Danny would bear
the brunt of Rosie's anger for asking her to cosign. Better to keep it
between them.

Now everything would have been just fine if Danny hadn't had a
hot streak at the racetrack. With money in his pocket, he wanted to
maximize his investment. So, he only made regular minimum payments to Etna while using the extra money to fund more trips to the
track. In other words, he was sandbagging.

Things were going just fine. In fact, Etna was so pleased with
Danny as a customer that they wanted to grant him additional credit. Well, back in those days, they didn't send you an email, they called
your house.

Guess who answered the phone on the day Etna called the house?
That's right, my Aunt Rosie. My uncle was once again in a jackpot but

not the kind he wanted. When he walked into the kitchen after work that day, my aunt mentioned he had a phone call.

"Oh, who was it?" he asked.

"Your Aunt Etna," she said.

"What did she want," he gulped.

"She said you finished in the money." And she held out her hand. My uncle filled it with all his winnings.

Red, Red Wine

S ometimes, there is a certain myth-like quality surrounding some
of the well-known stories in my family. Take my great grandfather Antonio for example — he was my Grandmother Margherite's father. Tonino they called him or "Little Tony." But what he
lacked in height he made up for in longevity — or so they say.

My grandmother used to love telling us this story. And if she told
us once, she told us a thousand times. Each time she'd start with the
same beginning. Whenever she poured herself a glass of red wine,
we knew what was coming.

It was hard for us not to roll our eyes or elbow each other in the
ribs. We knew the story so well; we'd often finish her sentences for her.

She'd say: "You know, your great grandfather lived to be..."

"One hundred and six!" Tony would interject.

She would stare daggers at him for stealing her thunder. I would
give him a dirty look.

And then she'd continue to extoll Little Tony's virtues — how
smart he was, how good he was at fixing things, and his skill at morra.

"And you know what he would drink every day since he was a
little boy?"

Carmen was about to open his mouth when I shook my head and
mouthed the word "don't."

Because to steal her thunder a second time would have meant a
schiafe to the head.

"Red wine," she said with an air of satisfaction.

And from here she moved on to the climax of her story, which we
all knew was coming.

But it gave her so much pleasure to come to the incredible con-
clusion of her story that we didn't dare interrupt her.

"And do you know how he died?" She asked.

We all knew how he died but that wasn't the point. The point was to be a good listener and ask.

"No, Nonna," I'd said as I made a face behind her back at Tony and Carmen. "How did he die?"

"He fell of off a roof he was fixing!" she concluded with pride.

A Salut!

Talking Turkey

We were talking about pets the other day. I have a rescue dog called Ernie. He's deaf, blind and he doesn't bark. Being deaf myself, we make quite a pair. In our house, when my children were young, we had our fair share of cats, dogs, kittens, turtles, goldfish, and mice. When asked about my pets, I often think of Tommy, our pet turkey.

Tommy didn't start out as a pet. When Tony, Carmen and I were young, we asked for a live turkey one Thanksgiving. Little did we know that later in the week Tommy would come to live in our cellar and become our friend.

Tommy was a clever bird. He could always sense when we were about to sneak down the stairs. He'd hide underneath the stairs to lie in wait, ready to chase us.

We'd creep down oh so quietly, first Tony and then Carmen. I would bring up the rear. We'd get to the bottom of the stairs and if there was no sign of Tommy we would call him.

"Gobble, gobble, gobble!"

He'd poke his head out and chase us to the stairs, where we would fall over each other trying to escape his sharp beak. Tony and Carmen would run right over me in their effort to get away. Thanks, guys!

Naturally, we were quite concerned that Tommy was going to be our guest of honor at dinner. We made my mother promise that we wouldn't eat him.

She agreed and said he would be sent to a farm where he could live outside and enjoy fresh air. (And here I confess, I may have used a similar explanation whenever the goldfish died, and we had to "free" them in the toilet so they could get to the ocean.)

When Thanksgiving Day arrived we were relieved that the bird on the table *wasn't* Tommy. As we sat at the table, my brothers, my parents, and my grandmother and I said a quick prayer of thanks. And just as my father was about to carve the turkey, Tony unbeknownst to us started to shake the table with his knee.

Carmen and I saw the turkey start to move, our eyes grew round, and we knew that Tommy wasn't on the farm. That he had come back to chase us and chase us he did. We ran out of the house screaming, "It's alive! It's alive!" And that was the last time we had a turkey as a pet.

Fuggedaboutit...

L ong before there was this popular and iconic phrase found in TV and on T-shirts there was an even better phrase created by my best friend, Nene.

Nene and I grew up together, and we were inseparable. Nothing bothered Nene, if she didn't like the job, she changed it. If her parents yelled at her for breaking curfew, she'd smile and shrug. Later in life she faced several health setbacks with the same calmness.

I should explain that Nene was a name we called each other. It was our shared code.

"Hey Nene, what do you want to do today?" I'd ask.

"I don't know, Nene. What do you want to do?" She'd reply.

I was thinking about Nene the other day as I walked through the neighborhood during the annual church festival. Everyone refers to it as The Feast.

As I passed the houses of friends and family past, I could see their faces. It was like watching a slow-motion movie. Some were waving, others were smiling, and others just nodded in recognition. Talk about watching your life pass before your eyes.

I once had a near-death experience, and I can say with confidence that that expression is true. Your life does pass before your eyes. And as I'm here with you today, all I can say is that God pushed the play button on my life, and my story continues. I think my mission is to share these stories with you.

And that's why I wanted to tell you about Nene, to share her words of wisdom. Her version of "fuggedaboutit" is what helps me get through some of my more challenging moments.

It's also a phrase I have shared with my children, my family, and my friends when they come to me with small problems that will eventually resolve themselves given time and detachment.

And that phrase is, "Whaddyagonna do, Nene? Whaddyagonna do?" In the end, nothing.

It's that kind of philosophy that leaves everything up to God. A God who pushes the play, pause, or stop buttons in our lives.

The Wheels of Life... Part 1

My life has always been closely tied to automobiles. Before I was officially licensed to drive, I was given lessons and practiced regularly in the narrow streets of our neighborhood. Occasionally when I was feeling bored or brave, I would venture farther afield unbeknownst to my parents and the local police.

Our neighborhood, although humble, boasted a large array of Cadillacs, Mercurys, and Buicks: big cars designed to make a big first impression, big cars made of American steel with fins, curves, and chrome. They looked good but drove like tanks, and I always felt safe behind the wheel. So did my passengers. That's because I had two very good teachers: my brothers Tony and Carmen.

Prior to taking my driver's test, I went out for a ride with them in Carmen's new Ford Roadster. It was a manual shift, two-seater but had a rumble seat in the back. As I'm petit, my brothers determined this was the perfect place for me.

We drove a few blocks and I grew bored. I really wanted to drive that car. I asked Carmen who promptly said "no way." Tony, always my champion, took my side and told Carmen to let me drive. I was ecstatic.

Carmen slid over to the passenger seat, Tony jumped in the back, and I got behind the wheel. I was cruising along Herman Avenue when Carmen decided that it was time to switch back and he ordered me to stop.

It was so unexpected that I hit the brake but forgot to put in the clutch and the car lurched forward to a stop but not before the momentum propelled Tony out of the rumble seat and into the front seat.

Tony yelled at Carmen, "Nice going, idiot! Whose bright idea was it to let her drive anyway?"

Once I mastered the art of driving a standard shift car, my services were called upon by my mother to take her to the grocery store. My brothers, who were never anywhere close by when she needed them, decided to give me a chance and asked me to drive her up the street to the local grocery store.

I was happy to do so, but the only car available was my father's brand new Cadillac parked in front of our house. The Cadillac was his baby, his pride and joy. And he parked it on the sidewalk next to a fire hydrant to ensure it was not dinged by the "lousy" neighborhood drivers. I wasn't sure, but my mother assured me it was okay because my father was at Bud's Bar and wouldn't be home for hours.

So off we went up the street to Fisher's Supermarket and everything went smoothly. As we shopped, we ran into several neighbors who were also at the market. Naturally, my mother offered them all a lift home in the Cadillac.

The car was full to bursting with neighbors, bags, boxes, and collapsible carts. It made backing out of the parking space difficult because I couldn't see. And as (un)luck would have it, I backed into another car.

When I got out to inspect the damage to the other car, the driver sensed my distress and reassured me that his car only had a scratch that he could buff out. Relieved, I continued our journey down West 69th street, dropping off passengers along the way.

As I pulled into the usual parking spot, I helped my mom with the groceries but not before noticing a huge dent on the side of the car. No wonder the other driver was so kind.

I panicked and said to my mother, "Dad is going to kill me. What am I going to do? I'm dead, I'll never get my license now, and I'll never get a car."

My mother, always a wise woman and three steps ahead of my father, told me not to worry. "Don't say anything. Let's see what happens."

Courtesy of Detroit Shoreway Community Development Organization.

A few hours later my father came home and burst into the kitchen. "Vee!! Vee!" He yelled for my mother. My mother came into the kitchen with a questioning look on her face.

"Yes, Teddy?"

"That's it! We're moving. I'm done with this neighborhood. Some *stunade* hit my car."

The Wheels of Life... Part 2

My career as a precocious driver didn't end with my trip to the grocery store. I only tell you these stories as a cautionary tale. Do as I say (get your license first) and not as I do — or did! Now that I'm older and wiser I can see the folly of my ways.

One night there wasn't a licensed driver to be found, and I had such a taste for a milkshake from the local diner. I decided to chance it. But not before stopping by to pick up my best friend Kay. She was "Thelma" to my "Louise."

There were no drive-throughs in those days. Back in the 1950s you pulled up, parked the car, and a waitress, sometimes on roller skates, came out to take your order. And then she would hang an aluminum tray on your door.

It was a nice summer night and Kay and I had the top down as we cruised into Diney's. Life couldn't get any better. That was until a police cruiser pulled in next to us and decided to order a bite to eat.

I had hoped they were only stopping by for Cokes. But no dice. They both ordered a meal. One looked over and nodded a greeting to us. I gave him my biggest smile and nodded back.

"What are you doing?" Kay elbowed me. "You're not supposed to call attention to us."

"Then they'll really think we've got something to hide," I hissed through a tight smile.

"Now what?" she asked.

"Drink slow."

And that's exactly what we did. We went through another two milkshakes before the police pulled away. And just for good measure, we waited for at least another two cars to leave before we left the parking lot. We must have set a Guinness World Book of Records that night for longest time in a diner's parking lot.

Silent Night

O nce I got my driver's license, I became the designated driver for many friends. I preferred driving to anything else.

I recall one Christmas Eve, I was celebrating with my friend, Kay, and her parents. Her dad, Charlie, retired early for the night. Kay, her mom, and I kept talking and eventually the conversation turned to the topic of Midnight Mass.

"And sure, wouldn't it be a good idea to go to Midnight Mass now," Kay's mom said.

But neither she nor Kay drove, and I didn't have my car that night. They decided that I would drive their family car. The only complication was that the sound of a starting car might wake Charlie.

"I know what we'll do," Kay's mom said cheerfully. "We'll push the car out of the driveway."

Their car was a big old Mercury. I think the two of them had had one too many glasses of sherry. I started to speak.

"How in God's name?"

"Precisely!" Kay's mom cut me off mid-sentence. "Just don't be takin' it in vain."

I'm not sure if it was thanks to the Almighty or the icy driveway, but when I put the car into neutral, it rolled silently into the street. It was a Christmas miracle. It was a cold silent night indeed.

Once the car hit the street, I turned over the ignition, and off we went to the Cathedral for what proved to be the longest Midnight Mass in history. By the time we got home it was 2:00 a.m.

Before they could object, I pulled into the driveway and killed the engine as quickly as I could. We all stared at the house. It was silent and dark, a sure sign that Charlie was still asleep.

An hour and a couple of glasses of wine later, visions of sugar plums began to dance in my head. I nodded off to sleep on the couch. But it wasn't long before all the lights came back on, the radio began playing Christmas songs, and Charlie woke us all up to attend early Mass.

So off we went, back to Mass — bleary-eyed, hung over and tired. But hey, better another Mass than a confession.

The Best Christmas Present

In Charles Dickens's story, "A Christmas Carol," Ebenezer Scrooge is visited by three ghosts: Past, Present, and Yet to Come. Lately, I've been visited by the ghost of Christmases Past. Not every Christmas was all merry and bright. Looking back, some of those Christmases are tinged with a bit of sadness, but I am no less thankful for them.

My mom, who was basically a single (but married) mother, raised us as best she could. My dad, who was in and out of our lives on an erratic basis, decided to make an appearance one Christmas Eve. He tapped on the kitchen window, a large giftwrapped box in his hands.

Back then, I was seven years old, and my brothers were only a few years older. We weren't quite sure how we felt about our dad. Tony and I opted for leaving him outside in the cold. Carmen, always the most sensitive of the three of us, and the oldest and the biggest, wanted to let him in. And because we loved Carmen, we gave in. Tony and I always gave in.

Dad didn't need to bring us presents when he came. His "presence" always meant more to us. But there it was, a beautifully wrapped box that begged to be opened. We tore at the wrapping paper and it revealed a Lionel Train Set. The boys were ecstatic. I was less so.

Tony, always sensitive to my moods, took a step back from the box and asked our dad, "Where's Louisa's present?"

To which he replied, "I didn't bring her one."

Tony took a step back, and told him. "In that case I don't want your present."

Carmen put the lid back on the box and handed it back to him.

Each brother grabbed one of my hands and led me out of the kitchen into the front room to play Checkers.

It was at that moment I realized that sometimes the best Christmas present is the one you don't get.

Amazing Grace

When coincidence and serendipity meet, good things happen. According to the dictionary, coincidence is a remarkable occurrence of events without an apparent causal connection. Serendipity one-ups coincidence because it adds happiness to the equation.

I remember one such meeting when I was in my teens. I was a regular at the Rollercade Skating Rink on Denison Avenue. Every Saturday afternoon most of the kids from the neighborhood went to skate dance. Sometimes we were lucky enough to win free tickets for admission. None of us owned skates so we had to rent them. I often wondered how many people had the skates on before me. But I didn't care. They had four wheels and a stopper, and I loved them.

Skating is truly an art form; it's like ice dancing on wheels. The Rollercade had live Wurlitzer organ music that you could skate to or, if you were good, dance to. You could skate along the outside of the center oval. If you were good you could skate/dance inside the oval. Skaters inside the oval could waltz, foxtrot, and flea hop.

Since I thought I was pretty good, I would skate inside the oval showing off a little here and there. Until one day a young woman showed up to dance with her partner. Anyone watching her skate knew that she was an angel on wheels.

From her beautifully pleated skating skirt and her blinding white skates to her elegant moves, she was everything I wanted to be as a skater. I was too intimidated to talk to her let alone skate in the oval with her. So, I sat and watched her for hours.

Who was she I wondered?

Well, it didn't take long before I found out.

One day I went to visit my Aunt Mary, and as was my habit, I burst into the kitchen with my usual enthusiasm only to find the skating angel sitting at the kitchen table writing a letter to her boyfriend.

I was dumbfounded. To say I was surprised was an understatement. I never thought I'd meet her let alone find her in my aunt's kitchen. I stood there with my mouth open as Aunt Mary introduced me to her friend, Grace. I told her how much I loved to watch her skate. She was very modest and kind as I complimented her skating, her clothes, and her skates.

A few days later my aunt gave me some skating skirts that Grace sent over. They were beautiful. I just knew that if I wore these skirts, I would be able to skate like Grace.

I met her again several months later when she was a bridesmaid in my aunt's wedding. She seemed to float down the aisle of the church. For a second, I wondered if she was wearing a pair skates under the floor length dress. No, I thought, it was probably just my imagination.

Many years later, I grew up and got married and moved back to the neighborhood. And I often wondered whatever happened to Grace. Well, I didn't have to wonder for very long because it turned out she was my neighbor. We became best friends and so did our husbands. We raised our children together and we taught them how to skate.

*

The Elements
of Style

I come from a long line of creative and resourceful women who could make something out of nothing at a moment's notice.

My mother was a milliner back in the day when everyone wore hats and gloves. I'm so sorry to have seen that element of style be replaced by today's more casual dress.

I was invited to a wedding in the 1960s and I wanted a new hat. So, my mother grabbed an empty Clorox bottle and cut out the bottom to create a form that fit perfectly on my head. She then wrapped a black tulle fabric around the form, fixing it in place with glue and fishing line. Once she had her base, she proceeded to glue little black and white feathers all around the crown. Soon she had a pillbox hat à la Jackie Kennedy. I made quite a statement when I paired it with a little black dress.

And speaking of dresses, my Aunt Rosie was a super seamstress when it came to poodle skirts for sock hops — especially on a moment's notice — which was just about all the time I gave her to pull one off. After a while, she wised up to "Last Minute Louisa" and kept fabric remnants, buttons, ribbons, and appliques handy in a kitchen cupboard.

To create the necessary poof of a poodle dress, sometimes Aunt Rosie used starched sheers (curtains) from her windows and overlaid them with a piece of cotton material, perhaps a tablecloth that she kept in her pantry. As she would pin the pieces in place — literally sewing them on me — she'd always tell me a story.

She and her five sisters were always impeccably dressed even as children. They may have not had much money back in the day (1920s); times were tough for this immigrant family. But they were always well turned out. My grandmother always made sure that their clothes were clean and mended and their shoes were polished. It was important to make a good impression. The Italians call it *Bella Figura*.

I marveled at her creativity and I asked her once if she had learned to be creative or if she'd been born that way. She laughed and said that it was a little bit of both. "Oftentimes," she would say, "necessity is the mother of invention, or the father of fashion."

Aunt Rosie can recall the first time she had to (literally) think on her feet one morning before going to school. She was in the fifth grade. She was already late when she put on a pair of socks that had been darned one too many times. The sock literally fell apart in her hands, so she grabbed a pair of scissors and snipped off the top of each sock, throwing the damaged bits away. She pulled the tops up to her mid-calf and slipped her feet into her high-top button shoes. The sock tops poked out of the shoes as usual. Perfect. No one would be the wiser. Or so she thought.

Everything was fine until the teacher announced that the class would have to go to the nurse's office for their annual physical check-ups. They would be weighed (without shoes!) and measured. After a good laugh all around, Aunt Rosie, who never took herself seriously, said that was the first step in a long career of stylish creativity.

All Hands On Deck

During our teenage years, our "part-time" father had a full-time job as a construction supervisor. When we'd saw his truck on West 69th street, we'd laugh amongst ourselves and say, "Here comes the money truck."

While we were happy that my mother would have some extra financial support, we were unsure about his daily presence in our lives. He tried to make up for lost time by buying each of the boys a car.

Dad bought Tony a Packard, which Tony promptly took apart and then reassembled. His interest stopped there because he was too laid back to drive. He'd rather be driven, lounging in the back seat of Carmen's new convertible. Carmen loved to drive, so it was a perfect match. As for me, I drove whatever car was in the driveway.

In exchange for the "wheels" and to pay for gas and insurance, my father put the boys to work with him on various construction sites. Where Carmen was an up-for-anything guy.

Tony was the opposite. Repeating the same task every day on the job site didn't do much for a boy who liked to see how things worked. Or perhaps it was just his rebellious nature; there was always a bit of friction between Tony and my father. It made no sense to Tony that my father could be so lax about his family and so exacting about a job. "You can't have it both ways," he once told me.

Convincing Tony to join Carmen and my dad became my mother's daily obsession. And no matter how much she begged, pleaded, threatened, or cajoled, Tony would just roll over and go back to sleep. She was the ultimate peacekeeper. But the best she could manage was an uneasy détente.

"Your father's going to be mad at you, Tony," she would cry.

One of the mornings Tony decided to sleep in, my father told him, "If you're not on the job today, you better not be here when I get back."

In a rare moment of obedience or rebellion — who can say — Tony took my father at his word, and that afternoon went out and enlisted in the Navy. At the time, my mother was angry at both her husband and her son. Later she grew to see the wisdom in Tony's move.

As for Tony, I think he liked the freedom of being away from home. In fact, he started a trend in the neighborhood. It wasn't long after Tony enlisted that Carmen joined the Air Force, my fiancé, Jimmy, joined the Army; slowly but surely all the boys joined the "service."

After Tony finished basic training, I received a postcard from California.

Dear Louisa,

The Navy is not bad. The food is not as good as at home. But I'm now a machinist first class which means I get to take a lot of things apart and reassemble them. The good news for the Navy is that there are no extra pieces left over when I put things back together, which means I must be doing something right. The bad news, I have to get up early every morning!

Love,
Tony

PS. Hope you're enjoying the Packard.

✍

The Little Drummer Girl

Whenever I hear the Christmas carol, "The Little Drummer Boy," I'm reminded of the time I marched in the drumline of Cleveland's West High School marching band.

The school was asked to participate in a parade that marched down Euclid Avenue for a civic holiday. I can't recall which one. What I do remember is how much I loved those band uniforms and how much fun I thought it would be to march in that parade.

In those days, joining the high school marching band was as easy as showing up and playing an instrument. Showing up was the easy part. Learning to play an instrument in a few weeks' time was a different story. I sought out the drum captain and convinced him to show me how to do it. He was skeptical at first. But he ended up showing me how to play a snare drum. To both our shock and surprise, I was a quick study.

It was the thrill of a lifetime to march in that parade. And it was a once in a lifetime performance, literally. That day marked the beginning and end of my promising career as a musician. But I got to keep the uniform!

Festival Season

The month of July is a very special month in the life of the neighborhood. It kicks off with the Fourth of July where we celebrate being Americans: Italian Style. In the 1950s and 1960s it was with pasta, and sausage and pepper sandwiches. Hot dogs and hamburgers only came into fashion in the 1970s.

It is also the feast of the local Catholic church where for five days everyone in the neighborhood came together to celebrate their heritage, raise money for the church and honor the patron of our church, Our Lady of Mount Carmel.

The best day was always Sunday, the last day of the Feast. After Mass, there was a procession with flower girls, altar boys, priests, nuns, and the various societies: Sacred Heart, St. Agnes, and Holy Name. The Knights of Columbus added a special touch with their exotic uniforms and shiny swords.

Leading the procession was a local marching band that played a wide variety of songs from religious and patriotic marches to sentimental Italian favorites.

The men in the neighborhood would get up early and open the fire hydrants to clean the streets to give the procession a clean place to walk. The tricolored flags of red, white, and blue, and green, white and red, hung as banners across the streets.

After the procession, I would treat myself and my children to a variety of carnival rides and games of chance. These were set up in the schoolyard behind the church.

From the top of the rickety old Ferris wheel, we could see our house two streets away. There were times when I thought a good stiff breeze would send it rolling down the schoolyard — The Ferris wheel — not our house.

In the old days, the schoolyard was packed with people from the neighborhood, visiting relatives, and friends from the "outside." There wasn't a face you didn't know directly or indirectly by way of aunts, uncles, and cousins.

Like most immigrant neighborhoods of the day, it was a close-knit community. There weren't very many outsiders, my Irish American husband being one of the exceptions.

He and his family stayed close to home near their Irish parish up the street. He used to joke about needing to know a secret handshake to get into our neighborhood, but he knew my brothers and that was good enough.

Even the president could have used a special introduction back in those days. Well, maybe not. Because when John F. Kennedy visited Cleveland in October 1962, and passed through our neighborhood in a motorcade, Detroit Avenue was jam-packed with well-wishers from all the local neighborhoods, waving and shaking his hand.

He even shook my Aunt Rosie's hand — after which she exclaimed, "I'll never wash this hand again!"

Even my two-year old daughter got in on the fun — held high by her father to see the passing president — she waved as if she knew him.

So much for the secret handshake!

That was a day the different neighborhoods dissolved, and everyone came together to celebrate as proud Americans.

~

The All-Inclusive Vacation

I saw this television commercial the other day for a ritzy all-inclusive Caribbean resort where everything was included. And I got to thinking about the popularity of such places. Back when my children were little, the term all-inclusive meant a full cooler in the trunk of the car and a trip to the local theme park.

When I was growing up, an all-inclusive vacation meant something else entirely. It was a euphemism meant for children or polite company. This all-inclusive vacation included clothing, food, phone calls, and a double room, unless you felt the need for a solitary space and your privacy. On this vacation, you could learn a trade and meet "friends" that could be useful when it came to networking.

There were more than a few people in the neighborhood who went "away" to these all-inclusive places. And they all came back with stories of colorful characters and capers. Those stories were carefully passed on to a select group of listeners. And despite my children's cajoling, you won't find any of them here with perhaps one exception: those involving my brother Tony. He used to tell me, "You can always learn by example, even the bad ones." Or as he liked to tell my children when they were growing up, "Do what I say, not what I do." So, although he may not have set a good example, he turned out to be a good influence.

Baby's First Christmas

Christmas Eve celebrations in Italian families are legendary for food, fun and, of course, faith. By faith, I mean a trip to church for Midnight Mass. But let's get back to the food. Except for an Italian wedding, you'll not see so much food at any other time.

It's a pescatarian feast with every kind of fish and seafood known to man. It's known as *Il Cenone di Vigilia*, the feast of the seven fishes, but there are often more than seven courses. In my family, everyone's favorite dish was always baccala, which is salted cod. And boy, could it stink up your house. You can imagine my Irish-American husband's reaction at his first Christmas Eve dinner *con la famiglia* at my mother's house.

It was also our first Christmas as a family. We had just had our first daughter, who was about nine months old at the time. And boy, was she energized by all the festivities. She sat on my lap watching the comings and goings of friends and family throughout the night. She ripped open presents, clapped, and sang. But she didn't eat a thing.

I knew that she was her father's daughter when she turned up her nose at every appetizer I put before her. My husband looked at her and nodded in sympathy as he waited for the main course of stuffed shrimp.

But my mother was adamant about not putting out any main dishes until my brother Tony arrived. After all, she said, this was "his day." Carmen, just finishing his second bowl of *calamari in brodo*, looked at her skeptically. It was getting late, and we were still waiting for the guest of honor. It was strange that he wasn't home yet.

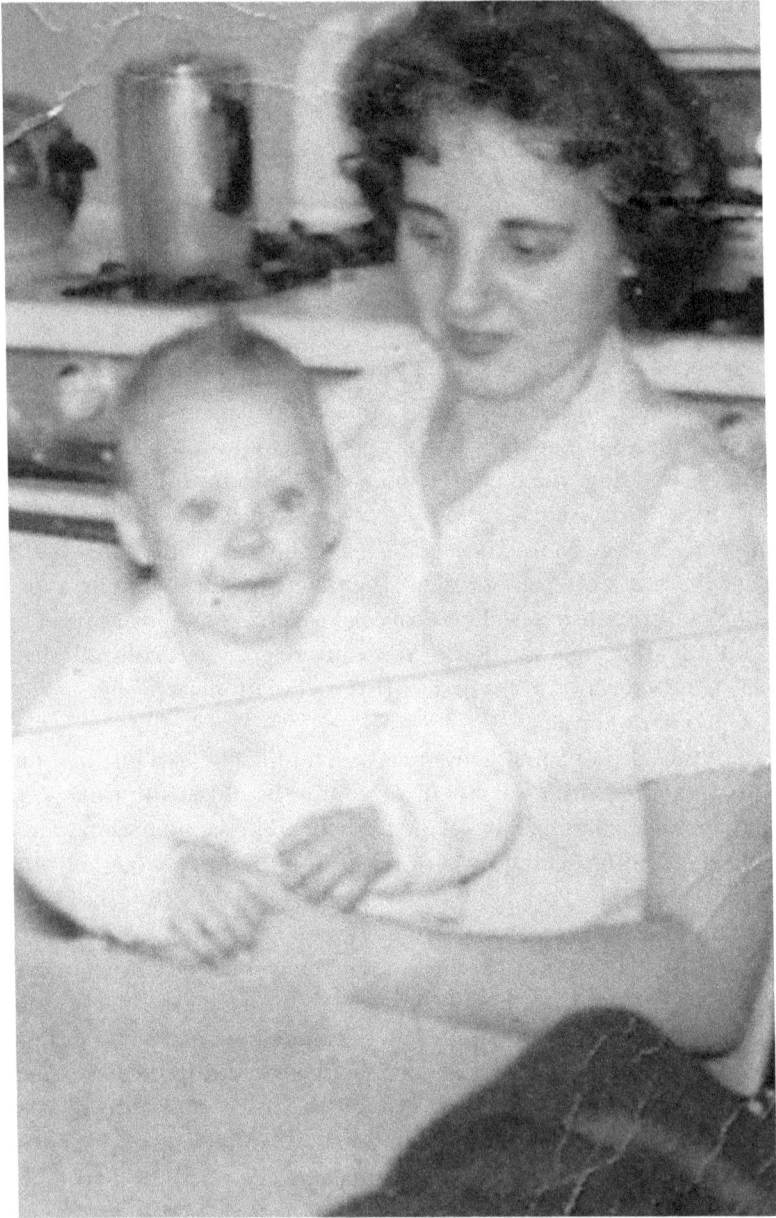

Just as we were about to dig into the main dishes, the front, back and side doors burst open. We all jumped as three men entered the house. I'd like to tell you they were the three wise men, but they weren't. They were Federal Marshals, wearing their six-pointed star badges. The irony of it made me laugh when I looked at the star on top of the Christmas tree.

Up until this time I had no idea that my brother was involved in anything other than floating craps games. My husband and brother Carmen were a bit wiser but thought it best not to worry me.

When the marshals asked my mother if she knew Tony's where-abouts, my mother was as stunned as I was. She said the first thing that came into her head: "Try church."

Satisfied that Tony was not in the house, the men left as abruptly as they'd arrived. But our *festa* was ruined. Tony was missing, and everyone was upset everyone except for my daughter who didn't have a clue about what had just happened.

Many years later she and I were talking about all the fuss that goes into making baby's first Christmas a special event. And even though she doesn't remember it, she laughs when she thinks about all the "fuss" of her first Christmas. And to make me feel better she likes to tell me, "I'd rather have a good story than some silly orna-ment that puts in an appearance once a year."

Her ability to shine a light on the positive could make anyone feel better. To me, she was and *is* my little Christmas star. Shine on!

The Safest Street in the Neighborhood

These days you can never be too careful when it comes to letting your children roam free. It seems like the dangers have multiplied tenfold since I raised my family in our little neighborhood. Back then, they walked to school by themselves (mind you, it was only three streets away.) They rode their bicycles to friends' houses or the playground. And so long as they called when they got to their destination, I didn't worry too much. Of course, we also had an "additional" layer of security unbeknownst to me, my children, and our neighbors. And I suppose I have my brother Tony to thank for that.

Tony worked for a "family business," and he was away a lot. He was the exotic uncle who traveled to "cool" destinations like Las Vegas, Miami, and Los Angeles. He dressed in flashy suits, wore Ray-Bans and drove a big Cadillac. And whenever he was in town, he spoiled my kids by showering them with time and attention. I guess today he would be called the "cool uncle."

When he was home, our house became a hive of activity. We had visitors coming in and out, and the phone never stopped ringing. And just as quickly as Tony would show up, he'd disappear again on another trip.

During those times when he would visit, we would have a few special visitors as well. Little did I know these visitors were *special agents* with the FBI, and they would sit outside of our house keeping an eye on it and an eye out for my brother.

It took me a while to realize that we had our own security. It wasn't until my children pointed it out to me that I figured it out. My oldest daughter noticed them right away. Every day on her way to and from school she'd wave to the smartly dressed men sitting in the parked car outside our house.

"Mom, they even wear ties," she said.

"Still," I said, "maybe they work for the city."

My son Jimmy then pointed out that the men were taking pictures of the street. And they seemed particularly interested in our elderly neighbor's house.

And so, I revised my opinion. "They must be realtors," I said.

When I approached our neighbor, Nanny, and asked her if she was moving, she just laughed and said, "Land sakes, no!"

And that's when the penny dropped. There was no need to bother the kids with any further explanations, so I was happy to let them believe that these visitors to our street were city workers or realtors.

That was until my middle daughter decided that anyone who spent so much time in a car certainly must be homeless. Being a good Christian child at Our Lady of Mount Carmel School, she did the only thing she could do to fix the sad situation. She walked up to the car one day, tapped on the window and invited them to live with us.

For the Birds

Earlier, I wrote a story called "The All-Inclusive Vacation." The story was written in jest but going away — or doing time — is hard. It's especially hard on the families that serve as a support network for people in jail. I know from first-hand experience because my brother Tony chose a crooked path. However, just because someone makes a mistake doesn't mean you can abandon them.

I'd go with my husband or my brother Carmen on cross-country trips to visit Tony who was "on vacation." That's how I explained it to my children when they were too young to understand. But they were hardly vacations.

I remember one visit. It was right around the time the movie *The Bird Man of Alcatraz* came out. We had all seen the movie, but we never thought we'd experience it. Until the day we walked into a visiting room filled with inmates and their families. It seemed like every inmate had a canary. The funny thing was that not one was chirping. I asked Tony why the birds were silent, and he looked at me, smiled, and said, "Smart canaries don't sing."

Carmen laughed. And I nudged Tony in the ribs, "Stop it, you mockingbird!"

We ended our visit by making light of a serious situation thanks to our fine feathered friends. Which reminds me of a poem by Emily Dickenson called "Hope is the Thing with Feathers." In it, she writes, "And sings the tune without the words/And never stops at all." And she was right!

However, in First Corinthians it's not hope but love that wins the day. "And now these three remain: faith, hope, love. But the *greatest* of these is *love*." While love may be the greatest thing, my mother never gave up hope that her prodigal son Tony would change his ways and come home to stay.

Years would come and go without him at the dinner table. As his mother, she loved him unconditionally and she always had faith that someday he'd surprise her and turn up on her doorstep. And occasionally, her faith was rewarded with a phone call from him to say that he was coming home. She would send me to the local butcher to buy the fatted calf: the biggest New York Strip in the shop. And then she would start to cook.

It was so nice to see my mother happy again. She always sang when she prepared his dinner because she never knew if this would be their last supper together before temptation beckoned and he disappeared again.

One day out of frustration, I asked my mother if she wasn't angry with my brother and his off again/on again life. "Louisa," she said. "I have two choices. I can waste my time being angry or I can spend my time with him in peace and love." She chose love.

✿

One More
From the Road

The Catholic Church considers visiting prisoners a Corporal Act of Mercy. It stems back to the early days of Christianity when Jesus, Peter, and Paul, as well as many early saints, were considered outlaws and imprisoned.

As Oscar Wilde once said, "Every saint has a past, and every sinner has a future."

I guess that's why, no matter where Tony ended up, we, my husband and I, would go and visit him. One such trip was the Atlanta penitentiary in the 1970s where he was doing time.

I guess when you have that much time on your hands, it gives you the opportunity to reflect on your life and the possibility of redemption. At least I know he did. That day, Tony promised me this would be his last "trip" and that when he returned home it would be to stay. But I knew given the kind of "business" he was in, that there was only one way out. You were in for life, or until you died. It made me sad to think about it.

He then changed the subject. At the time, there were lots of articles in the Catholic newspapers on a miraculous statue of the Weeping Virgin. I had longed to see it, but it was somewhere in Europe, and I put it out of my mind. To my surprised, Tony handed me a newly finished drawing he'd completed of the Weeping Virgin. It was beautiful to behold.

Several months after our visit to Atlanta, we learned the Weeping Virgin was coming to America. And not only that, but there was also a scheduled visit at our church. The priests selected my daughter, Margaret, to place a crown of roses on the Virgin's head. We were honored.

(Jimmy, my son, would also like me to mention that he was an altar boy at this Mass, head altar boy to be precise.)

Maybe it was because I saw the drawing of the Weeping Virgin while visiting Tony that I felt I had a personal connection with the statue. It made me think that, somehow, the Virgin was sent to watch over all her children — even the wayward ones.

Amen!

Hello Jesus!

I t's me, your friend Tony. I wanted to thank you for all the times you were there for me. Even though I couldn't see you, I could always feel your presence. You never left me. And believe me there were times when I wouldn't blame you if you did.

You always believed in me. The problem was I never believed in myself. You knew there was hope for me, but I never realized it until it was almost too late.

You see there were lots of near misses and different roads that were often dead ends, but each was like a puzzle piece in my life. Sometimes the pieces fit, and other times not. And, for as much as I like to think I was putting all the pieces together, it was really You. You oversaw the creation of the big picture we call life.

Speaking of pictures, I made my own painting of You, Mother Theresa, and Padre Pio. It is always with me, either folded up in my pocket or in a frame at "home," wherever home was.

The picture only represents a story for me. The reality is that You are my friend. You shared that bumpy road of life with me, the ups and downs. Some beautiful places, some not.

In the end, You taught me how to love. "Love one another as I have loved You," You said. The wave of Your love washes over me and buoys me up. It was on this wave of that love that You called me home on that fateful day in April 1985.

"Hello, Tony, it's Your friend, Jesus," you said. "And it's time to come home."

Within the drawing, the following text appears:

Shroud
✝
Angel of
1916
Portugal
O my God, I
believe in,
I adore, I
hope in
and I love
you
✝
Matthew
25:35,36
By Ted Ricci
Padre Pio
Mother Teresa

There isn't a day that doesn't go by that I don't think of Tony. The picture he drew is in my kitchen. It keeps me company. It reminds me that even on my worst day I have a friend watching over me, helping me move those puzzle pieces into place.

Lost and Found

As you can see from the previous stories, sometimes people get lost. But with time, and enough love and understanding, sometimes they can also find themselves in a better place than where they started. They once were lost but now are found that's amazing grace for you.

My husband and I always tried to keep an eye out for lost children. Lord knows we certainly had enough practice with our seven. Experience had taught us that sometimes all it took was a kind word or sympathetic ear to keep people on the right track. And, on occasion, as my sons and their friends would attest, a swift kick in the pants or a *sciafe* to the head is sufficient motivation.

I remember one story about a young man who found himself in some difficult financial circumstances. One day he stopped by our house and tried to sell us a pair of new athletic shoes. Knowing his situation, it wasn't difficult to guess how he'd found the shoes.

When my husband Jimmy asked the young man where he got the shoes, he said he found them. Jimmy told him he would *buy* them on one condition, that the young man put them back where he found them. The young man agreed.

You're probably thinking "what's to stop the young man from selling the shoes again to someone else?" Well, here's where the psychology kicks in.

Jimmy said to the young man, "I want you to know that this is the best ten-dollar investment I have ever made."

And you know what? It was. That boy grew up to be a fine young man and every time I see him, I couldn't be prouder.

It Doesn't Cost Anything

My husband used to say, "It doesn't cost anything to be nice." And he was right. He walked the talk his entire life. Whether he was buying lunch for some stranger down on his luck or giving our income tax return to some less-fortunate family until they got back on their feet. He was always glad to do it. And most of his good deeds went unseen.

My daughter just told me one such story. Over breakfast a few months ago, a few of her male classmates from her grade school years were talking about her dad. It was their final year (Eighth Grade), and none of the boys had made any steps toward filling out their high school applications.

The boys told her that one day they were playing football in a field when my husband drove by and stopped to watch a few plays. He then inquired about their future studies. There was a long pause. They were a bit embarrassed.

He was a bit concerned to say the least. He also sensed an opportunity to promote his local alma mater, the all-boys Catholic High School that he helped to "build." (Build is a bit misleading. He dug the foundation as part of his after-school detentions. But that's another story.) He was a proud graduate of St. Edward's and if he could steer the next generation that way, he would be happy knowing that they would get a first-rate education.

He took charge and told the boys to meet him back at the field the following Saturday. He wanted them showered, shaved, and dressed in suits and ties. He drove them to an open house at St. Edward's where they all signed up. Like his own children, I don't think he gave them much choice. And I really don't think they minded one bit.

Later, when they all grew up, some of them had sons of their own who also attended the same high school. Occasionally, when he'd bump into those boys (I should them call men), Jimmy would beam like a proud parent.

It was a small act of kindness that cost nothing but meant the world to him.

The Shoes Off His Feet

M y children inherited the same kindness and sensitivity gene as their father. Some people give the shirt off their back; the year Jimmy, my son, was eleven, he gave the shoes off his father's feet. But luckily his father wasn't wearing them at the time.

My husband, Jimmy had two pairs of shoes: the shoes he wore every day to work, with pieces of cardboard covering the holes in the soles. And a second pair he wore to church, weddings, and funerals. The "good" shoes.

One bitterly cold November day, our eleven-year-old son came home from school quite concerned. There was a hobo at the bus stop who had no socks, and the shoes he had were falling off his feet.

Knowing that there was a perfectly good pair of shoes just sitting in the closet, our son grabbed the shoes and ran back to the bus stop to give them to the poor soul. The hobo then thanked him before he boarded the number 26 bus heading west.

Well, everything was fine until Sunday morning rolled around and we all got up for church.

"Louise," my husband yelled, "Where are my good shoes?"

"In the closet where you always leave them," I responded.

"No, they're not."

That's when our son piped up and proudly informed us that he had given the shoes away.

I could feel Jimmy's blood pressure rise a notch or two. But what could he do? In his heart, he knew he would have done the same thing. Like I always told him: if the shoe fits.

In Mom We Trust

've always encouraged my children to use their heads and make good choices. I trusted them and they rarely disappointed me.

I used to keep ten single dollar bills underneath a dish in the cupboard. They only used the money to put gas in their cars, buy treats, or pay for some school supplies. But I always told them: "Take only what you need because someone else might need the money too."

My son Jimmy was especially good at following that rule. He took my advice and only spent what he thought he needed on gas. He could have filled the gas tank, but he didn't. He only put enough gas in his used Karmann Ghia, to get him to and from school. Some days he would roll into his usual curb spot in front of the house on nothing but fumes.

Then one night someone stole his car. A thief tried to take more than he needed and didn't get very far. He only got as far as the bottom of the street before the car ran out of gas. Luckily for Jimmy, he took my advice and only spent what he thought he needed on gas. He could have filled the gas tank but he didn't. The thief tried to take more than he needed and didn't get very far.

Danny Thomas once said, "There are two kinds of people in the world: takers and givers. Takers may eat better but the givers sleep better."

Secret Signals... Hooty Hoo

Based on the title of this story you may be thinking it's about the sound a hoot owl makes on a moonlit night as you walk through a deserted wood. But it's not as scary as it sounds. It's a secret code developed between me and my son, Jimmy, when he as six years old.

You see, we lived on a busy street with lots of traffic. It had at least four factories which meant lots of employee and semi-trailer truck traffic. It could be very dangerous, especially for little boys chasing baseballs, footballs, and basketballs on their way home from school.

And so out of a sense of caution and instinct, I instructed Jimmy to call me before he crossed the street.

"Hey mom! Hey mom!" He would yell. And I'd push open the screen door and watch him look both ways. And then he'd dash across the street.

One day, he came to me and expressed concern about what his friends would think if they ever saw him calling his mother to cross the street. I could tell he had given this issue some serious consideration.

I asked him what he would like to do instead. He said that he'd like to have a secret code instead of yelling. In my mind, yelling to get your mother's attention, no matter what you said, was going to draw stares, but he said it wasn't what you said that mattered but how you said it.

I had to agree with him there. And so, on those days when he stood at the curb of our busy street all by himself, he puffed himself up like an owl and cried "Hooty Hoo! Hooty Hoo!"

The first time he did that our neighbor Nanny happened to be coming out of her house at the same time I opened the door. She looked at Jimmy, and she looked at me, and said with a wink, "Why land sakes, Louise! It sounds like we have an owl in our neighborhood."

And with that, Jimmy flew across the street back home to the nest.

Happy Mother's Day! To All the Belle le Mamme

By my grandson, Dominic Kennedy

This is a poem from my grandson, Dominic Kennedy, celebrating his mother's birthday. With a couple of adjustments, I thought it would make a nice Mother's Day poem to mammas everywhere!

It's Mother's Day today.
And I wouldn't have it any other way
Because I get to spend it with you.
Surrounded by your favorite crew.
Dad is lucky to call you his wife.
And I am eternally grateful that you're in my life.
You really are my favorite roommate
Because with your help I know I can be great!
Hanging with you, I know I'll never be bored.
You and me, we are in constant accord.
You are the one that told me to always love the Lord,
When it comes to faith you have given me St. Michael's sword.
When it comes to your day, I hope it is blessed,
Because when I'm with you, I am never stressed.
I love you mom, and I think you're the best!

It's (Not)
My Party...

Recently I had a chat with my daughter-in-law Anna about her Italian upbringing in the 1970s and the strict rules of mourning she had to follow. As an adult, she can look back and laughingly tell the tales of a perplexed American child who, at the age of six couldn't celebrate Christmas one year because of a death in the immediate family even though it was back in the old country! No Christmas tree and no *festa*. Her mother wore black for a year. And she cried.

Fast forward a few years, she was about to celebrate her First Communion, complete with a fluffy white dress and a family party. That was until another death in the family cancelled the party just days before the event. The party invitations were withdrawn. Her mother wore black. She cried.

Naturally, when it came time to graduate from high school, my daughter-in-law didn't get her hopes up for a party. And it's a good thing she didn't! Her mother wore black. She cried.

A week before the biggest event of her life, her wedding, my own mother, Vincenza, died. Given my mother's views on mourning, I knew she would want the wedding to go on. And it did. This time when my daughter-in-law cried, it was tears of joy.

✍

No Such Thing As the Perfect Crime

By now you may have already read the story, "The Bus Stops Here." It's about the time my two brothers "borrowed" a bus and ended up before a judge. Fast forward 30 years later, and I had my own jailhouse experience with my own two sons. Away at college, they found themselves in a minor scuffle with the football team during the wee hours of the morning.

The campus police hauled them and the team to jail and then into night court, where they stood before a weary local judge. My two sons chose to defend themselves. That makes me think of the old expression "A man who is his own lawyer has a fool for client."

However, they were successful because neither I nor their father heard about it until several months later. There was no late-night call for bail money, no time served, and nothing other than a mention in the local campus newspaper's police blotter.

The perfect crime, or so they thought. Until the holiday break when my husband happened to run into a woman whose son attended the same college. She was happy to share the news with him. Our sons were famous, or infamous depending on how you saw it. They had even made the school paper.

My husband listened with great interest and affected an air of gravity. He kept his cool. "Yes, yes, this was very serious," he said. "Of course, he knew all about it. Tut, tut..."

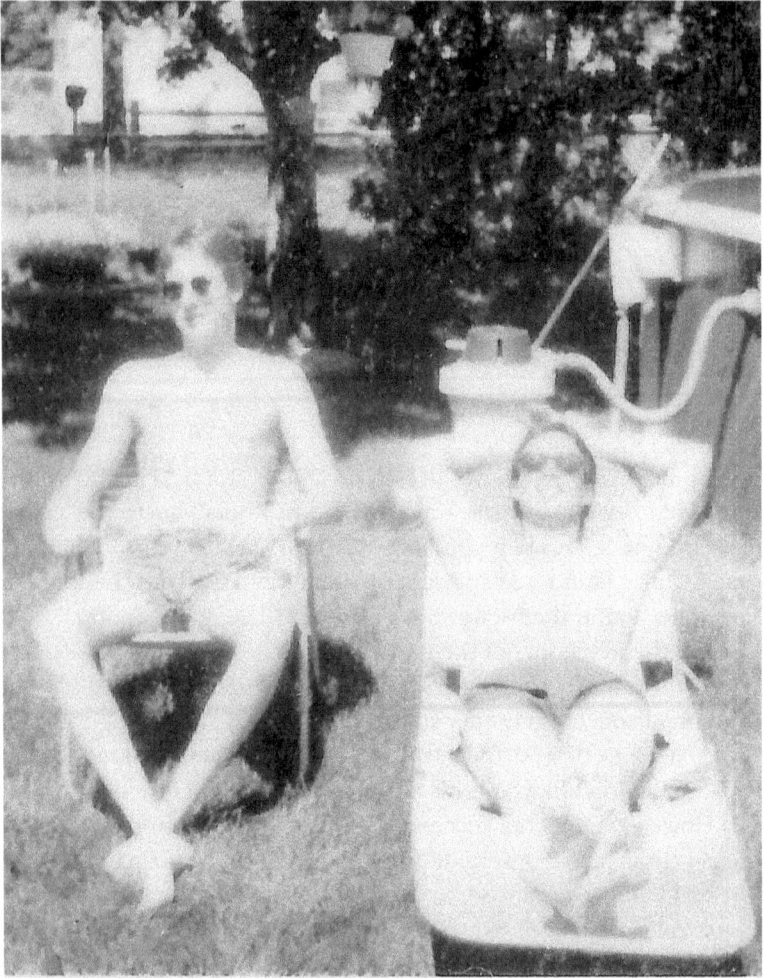

A week later, during the Thanksgiving prayer, my husband ended the Grace prayer with "And lead Jimmy and Michael not into temptation and deliver them from fighting. Amen."

In the words of my sons: "Busted!"

Showtime!

By my oldest daughter, Catherine

When it came to nurture, my salesman father, who worked in the grocery business, made sure to instill enough confidence in his brood so we'd be comfortable in any situation, whether it was meeting new people or speaking in front of a crowd of strangers.

He did this by instituting "The Show," a nightly after-supper performance ritual in which the four older children, ages 5 through 14, got up to perform while the three young preschoolers looked on in happy amazement at the spectacle unfolding before them. To prove there was nothing to it, my father joined in. We were our own reality show, only we didn't know it. "This Family's Got Talent," my father would probably have called it.

Our stage was just in front of the television, and the nightly prize was one dollar, which was a lot of money in those days. Every night before the performance, my father made a big show of taking a dollar bill out of his wallet and laying it on top of our large Magnavox console TV.

It was always a new dollar, crisp and clean. He'd rub it between his thumb and forefinger to make sure there was only one. We coveted the prize, each of us fantasizing about what treats and treasures a dollar could buy us at the local dime store.

The winner was determined by the loudest applause from the audience. Strategically we clapped the loudest for ourselves and tepidly for the "competition."

As the oldest I went first and I usually recited a scene from a play, perfecting acting skills never to be used professionally but handy nonetheless. I was a modern-day Portia pleading her case before a jury: "The quality of mercy is not strained. It dropeth as the gentle rain from heaven."

My mother would lick her finger, touch my temple and, making a hissing sound, draw her hand back quickly as if she'd burned it with a hot iron. "How did you ever get to be so smart? It sure wasn't from me." That compliment was better than a dollar any day, since my mom was one of the smartest people I knew.

My brother Jimmy, looking every bit as Italian as my grandmother with his dark hair neat and clean in a crew cut and his shining, big brown eyes, sang the very sad Irish ballad "The Wild Colonial Boy." It's about an Irish immigrant who leaves his home in Ireland and travels to Australia, where he meets a tragic end. I could never figure out if Jimmy's voice cracked with the emotion of the song or because he had just turned 13 and was, according to my mother, "at *that* age."

Next up was my sister Margaret Mary, whose new bellbottom pants were quickly turning into floods. (The quintessential middle child, she inherited the tall gene from my Irish grandparents.) At ten years of age, and with an unruly mop of long brown with bouncy spiral curls, and big blue eyes, she looked like a gangly Shirley Temple. Dancing lessons would have helped her, but they were a luxury we couldn't afford. But that never stopped her. She was a master of improvisation.

And then there was Michael, a five-year-old redhead with blue eyes and an endless supply of jokes, some that made sense and others that did not. They at least made him laugh. And, when Michael laughed, he laughed with his whole body, and that made us laugh.

I'm not sure if there is anything better or worse than performing in front of the hoots and heckling of your own family. Who better to knock you down a peg or two than those people who know you best, who know your weak spots and who may want revenge for some previous day's transgression, like eating all the Oreos? Then again there's no better training ground for bouncing back and developing a thick skin: two essential life skills that have served all of us well.

"Hey Dad," Jimmy would yell during one of Margaret's dances. "You should make her register those arms as lethal weapons."

Dad is still winning the dollar after all these years!

"Hey Jim," I would retort. "Maybe if you win the dollar you can get yourself some singing lessons."

And my mother would sigh: "So much for love and harmony," she'd say to my grandmother. "This is more like Friday night at the fights."

The last person to perform was my dad. Slight of stature and whippet thin, with curly brown hair and bright blue eyes, he was a natural entertainer and storyteller. He also had a beautiful voice. He always sang a few lines of a rather silly song, an old playground rhyme called "Ms. Mary Mack," but he called it "The Elephant Song."

I asked my mother for fifty cents
To see the elephant jump the fence.
He jumped so high,
He reached the sky.
And never came back till the Fourth of July.

The applause from his adoring audience was thunderous. It was clear who the winner was that night and *every* night because we were all too selfish and stupid to support each other on a rotating basis. We were all eternal optimists who were certain that the next time would be our turn to win the dollar. In the end, even with no green in our pockets, it was our colorful childhood that made us winners.

♫

What Are You Thankful For?

woke up this morning feeling a little blue thinking about all the people who are no longer with us. Of course, mine is not a unique situation; everyone will miss someone dear this holiday season. So rather than dwell upon who was missing, I decided it was better to think about what we did; the memories we made, and the good times we had.

Whenever I want to make myself smile, or even laugh, I think back to those early days we spent at the beach, otherwise known as Edgewater Park.

There were three ways to get to the beach. The first way was to cross the railroad tracks at the bottom of our street and then carefully make your way down a steep hill that was covered in trees and shrubs. Miss one step and you'd arrive with a skinned knee — guaranteed.

Once we landed on the beach, we'd set up camp. No one had beach chairs; instead, we spread blankets on the sand and ate lunches out of a picnic basket. Kids would dive headfirst into giant waves only to find that when the waves quickly rolled back, they had faceplanted into the sand. It didn't take long for us to learn that Lake Erie is a shallow lake.

Fleets of cyclists, with refrigerated coolers of ice, pedaled up and down the beach selling Checker Bar ice cream. One bar cost a quarter. Eating ice cream on the beach was rather messy, and you often ended up eating some sand as well.

Lake Erie got me to thinking that people are a lot like waves. They come, and they go. But memories just like the lake are always there.

Courtesy of Detroit Shoreway Community Development Organization.

And so, for the people who will be with us during the holiday season and even those who won't, I'd just like to say, "Thanks for the memories."

𝒢

Love Springs Eternal

By my son, Michael

It was the spring of 1986, and I was at a keg party at Ohio University. There were plenty of those back in the day but this one was different. What made it different was this pretty blond girl: the kind of girl who would be at ease whether she was drinking beer in a pub or sipping champagne in a palace.

I wasn't looking for a girlfriend, but there was something about her. Her name was Andrea, and I fell hard. We made some small talk, but not much happened. After all, it was a keg party.

Still, I remember telling my buddy, Mike, "The Truth," Townsend, "I'm going to marry that girl one day."

"Good plan," Townsend said. "Just one minor complication. She has a boyfriend."

That's the situation for now, I thought, but this is college, and maybe one day she won't be in a relationship and then I can ask her out.

Over the next few months, I would see her around because she lived in the same housing complex as my Ultimate Frisbee teammates. Yeah, Ultimate Frisbee was an actual college club sport.

With spring and Frisbee season behind me, I headed back to Cleveland for the summer. I worked at Boehm's sheet metal company on 73rd street, hung out at Art's place, the local Italian Club where I caught up with my friends from the neighborhood. But I couldn't get Andrea off my mind.

Summer melted into fall, and I moved back to Ohio University. First day back, who do I run into in the elevator of the building we both were living in?

She said, "I know you."

"I know you too," I said. This time I wasn't as talkative because there was no keg.

Later, I asked a mutual friend about Andrea's relationship status, and he thought she wasn't seeing anybody. I told him to make sure because I didn't want to interfere. He came back and confirmed that she wasn't seeing anyone.

For our first date, I asked her to go to the movies and, incredibly, she said "yes." We went to see *ET* at the Frontier Room. It was free, and they served beer. (Work-Study money only went so far in those days, so I had to be creative.)

We were going out for a few months when I thought it was time for Andrea to meet my family. After all, I had already met hers. I will tell you; I was little nervous because as you know from reading my mom's stories, anything is possible with my family.

So, we drive up to my parent's house, and everybody was there: my parents, all my siblings and my grandmother, who also lived with us. They regarded me with great skepticism. They thought I would never settle down.

My brother Jimmy, being Jimmy, kept calling Andrea "Adrianne." My dad asked if she needed glasses. My mother and grandmother were gracious and warm, offering food, drinks, and so on. My younger siblings were out doing their thing with their friends but not before stopping by to check out the "girlfriend."

All in all, the weekend was a success. There weren't too many embarrassing stories about me, and Andrea didn't flee in the middle of the night.

Sunday morning came around, and it was time for church. As we got up to go to Mass, Andrea sat at the kitchen table looking relaxed and wondering where we were all going.

Jimmy asked, "Aren't you going to Mass?"

Andrea said, "No, I'm not Catholic, I'm Methodist."

Everything just stopped. It got so quiet in the kitchen you could hear the clock ticking on the wall.

I thought *uh oh*, here we go. I was the first in the family to bring home a girlfriend who was not Catholic, and that was a big step, or so I thought. Leave it to my grandmother, in her infinite wisdom, to find an answer.

"That's okay," she said. "Catholic, Protestant, Jewish: we all play for the same coach."

Amen, I thought.

That was over 30 years ago. It wasn't long after that Andrea became my beautiful wife. Oh, and one more thing.... We were married in a Methodist church. *Amen*.

Lesson Learned

There's no such thing as perfection. Every family has its fair share of suffering and challenges. And we're no different. My brothers and I caused a great deal of heartache for my amazing mom. She always stood by us and held our hands along life's path, despite the twists, turns, and detours.

And then there are my children who are responsible for every single grey hair on my head. And while they grew up to be amazing adults, there were times when they were no angels.

Back in the day, I only had one rule: you had to finish high school. I figured one step at a time as I accompanied them on their journey. The college discussions would have to come later. Take my son, Jimmy, for example. He was a bright but bored student. To get him to turn up at his high school classes took some doing. So, I made it very simple.

I said, "If I can't trust you go to school then it looks like I'll just have to go with you. And I will sit next to you."

It's funny the things that will motivate a kid. Needless to say, he went on to graduate high school, without his mother in tow, and he moved out on his own soon after he graduated.

Having helped him clear one hurdle, I casually mentioned college.

"College? You said all I had to do was graduate high school," he exclaimed.

"I lied," I said.

But I thought I'd also give him a little leeway. So off he went to live with a roommate three streets away. I remember telling him that he had my blessing. His father had another opinion entirely which I cannot print here. Jimmy lasted three months before he ran out of money and called to ask if he could come home.

And I said, "Of course!"

He then said that he'd move back in two weeks after he got back from a trip to Florida.

"Florida? He had money to take a trip to Florida but not pay rent?" I asked. His logic baffled me. But it wouldn't be the first time.

My husband always had an age limit for how long the kids could stay at home. It was 54 years old. When Jimmy came back home to live, I was thinking he just might hit the age limit.

It took Jimmy awhile to make his way to college. There were lots of stops and starts and bumps in the road. But he finally got on track and went first to community college and then university. He graduated with honors and I didn't even have to threaten him.

And you know, it's the oddest thing. For a boy who didn't like to go to class. He became a teacher. He went from learning lessons to teaching them!

The Shoe Is On the Other Foot

I n this book, you'll find a story called the "Shoes off His Feet." In brief, it was a story about how my son gave away his father's best pair of shoes to a homeless man.

Fast forward, a couple of generations later, and I'm happy to report that the tradition of kindness continues in our family. My grandson, Pat, who lives out of state, called me the other day to chat and he told me this story.

While stopped at a traffic light, Pat saw a man who was poorly clothed for the cold weather. And to complicate his plight, the man had only one shoe. What happened to the missing shoe? One can only imagine.

My grandson rolled down his window and asked the man what size shoe he wore. The man responded size 10. As luck would have it, my grandson had the same shoe size. And so, he took off his left shoe and handed it to the man and drove off.

He drove about half a mile before realizing that he should have given the man both shoes — a matched pair. I guess in the heat (or in this case the cold) of the moment, he just reacted instinctively to helping someone as best he could. Realizing his error in judgement, Pat drove back to where he last saw the man, but he was gone.

Somewhere in Charlotte, North Carolina there's a poor man running around with mismatched shoes but warm feet. As for my grandson, the shoe is literally now on someone else's other foot.

As you've seen from some of these stories, what my family sometimes lacks in logic they make up for in kindness.

Post-Christmas Blues

It seems like I've been focusing a lot on my sons at the expense of my four amazing daughters. And since it's Christmas time, I'd like to share with you one of my favorite stories.

As every parent knows, it's children who add the magic to Christmas. My husband, my mother, and I would stay up till three or four in the morning assembling and wrapping gifts. That may seem late to you, but keep in mind we have seven children. That's a lot of wrapping paper! Also, my husband was not exactly a handy man with tools. He put everything together using a butter knife.

We barely got to sleep before three little people burst into our room ready to open presents. It was my three younger children, Danny, Beth and Donna, their ages ranging between two to five years old. The other four kids, the older ones, made up the balance of the sleepy conga line that snaked its way down the stairs, through the living room and into the den where piles of presents awaited them.

Bah who could sleep anyway? I thought. I was as excited as they were. After all, I had picked the perfect gifts. If there's one thing I know, it's my kids. Or so I thought.

In a matter of minutes, the floor was waist deep in wrapping paper, boxes, and bows. My children were busy playing, riding their bikes, or trying on clothes, all except for one. Beth had disappeared from the den. We eventually found her in the dining room sitting in a laundry basket crying. I was worried. Did I miss something? Did I buy the wrong thing? Didn't she like the Mrs. Beasley doll?

She did not! She was sure she had told Santa she wanted Dressy Bessy.

"You can't dress Mrs. Beasley," she cried.

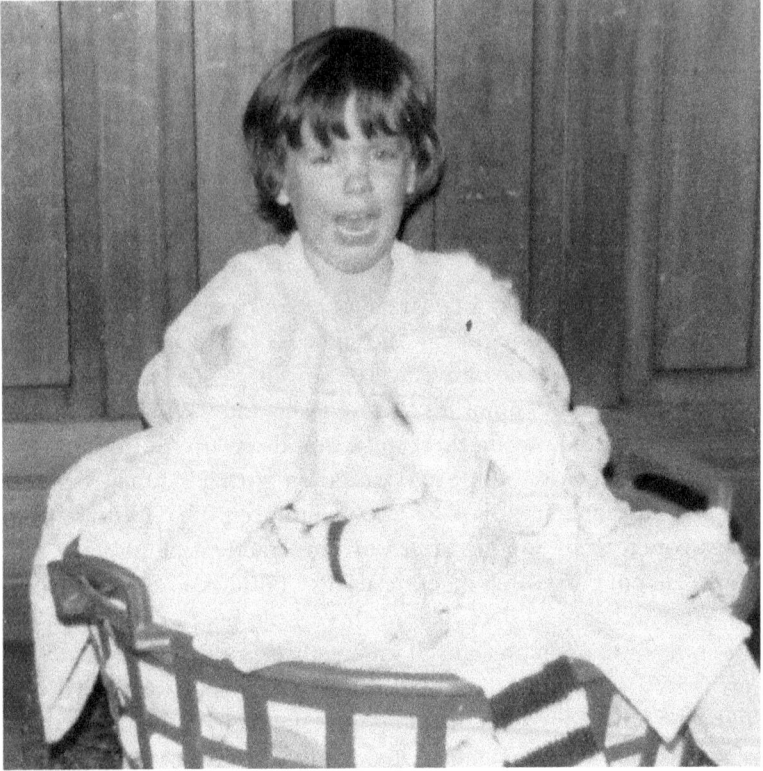

"Oh yes, you can," I said. "We can dress her plenty if you just get out of the laundry basket!"

A Moo... ving Story

When my kids were young, we didn't take many vacations. Most of our adventures occurred daily in and around our neighborhood. We took short trips to visit relatives; we drove along Edgewater Drive and admired the stately houses with the wide lawns. Or we over drove to Agozzino's Kustard Stand and had ice cream.

Our ritual upon returning to West 73rd Street was always the same. When we reached the top of the street, all of the kids started to chant: "Down the lake! Down the lake!"

That was the signal for my husband to bypass our house and continue driving to the bottom of our dead-end street where we parked in front of the railroad tracks and rolled down the windows waiting for the trains to pass. Each of my children tried to guess the color of the caboose. There was a lot of flailing and yelling if someone called out the exact color as his or her brother or sister.

My husband's response was always the same. "Don't make me turn around there, or I'll caboose you."

Most guessing games ended peacefully with everyone waving frantically at the flag man, who always managed to poke his head out of the back door of the caboose and wave back.

I am amazed at the simple things that brought such delight to my kids. Even a trip up 65th Street to the stockyard was an adventure. Not as much for my kids as it was for the cows.

I mean how many cars full of kids pull up to a cattle pen and *moo*? My daughter likes to joke that the weekly trip to the stockyards was as close as we were going to the country. And she was right.

I remember one time Jimmy, my son, asked if he could get out of the car and pet the cows.

And my husband said, "Jimmy, can't you read that sign on the fence?"

"Sure!" Jimmy said proudly. "Closed to the public."

"Well, there you have it, son. Closed to the public," my husband repeated for emphasis

But Jimmy quickly responded, "That's okay, Dad. We're Catholic." Holy Cow!

And She'll Have Fun, Fun, Fun...

By now you may have already read another story in this book called "Baby's First Christmas." Well, the baby in that story quickly grew up and wanted to learn how to drive. She took lessons after school, got her learner's permit, and tried to practice as much as possible before taking her driving test.

One Sunday, my husband, who I should add wasn't the most patient man, offered to take her driving in Sears's parking lot. Back in those days, the stores were closed on Sundays so there was no danger of her hitting anyone or anything.

My daughter is a lot like her father in many ways including her lack of patience and Irish temper. But who could blame her: she's a redhead, and the oldest of seven, who just likes to "get things done." I wasn't sure how this combustible mix of personalities was going to work out especially without me there to referee.

Now mind you, I wasn't there, so no one really knows the truth. But from what I gathered my husband didn't like the way my daughter was driving. Or, my daughter didn't like the way my husband was supervising. In any case, my husband wanted to take over the wheel. He got out of the car expecting my daughter to relinquish the wheel.

Unfortunately, he never got the chance. Just as soon as he closed the passenger door and walked around the rear of the car, my daughter took off, leaving her father stranded in Sears's parking lot. The store was several miles away and there were no cell phones back in those days.

Naturally, when she pulled into the driveway without him I could guess what had happened. So I went into rescue mode and told her to go and stay at her grandmother's and don't' come home until I called her.

My daughter handed me the keys. And then I went and picked up my husband who had managed to cool down enough to laugh about it on the ride back. "It will be a long time before she sees these again," he said jingling the keys. I guess he got the last laugh.

Grandma, You've Got Mail

In this fast-paced world of texts, Instagrams, and emails, getting a handwritten note is a rarity these days except for special events (graduations, weddings, communions, etc.). Most good wishes and greetings have gone digital. Digital missives would be very convenient especially for me who's usually late when it comes to sending out birthday cards to my children and grandchildren. The only problem is I haven't a hot clue how to do any of these digital things.

Birthday wishes are always preceded by a phone call and my signature closing: "Happy Birthday, I love you, and the card is in the mail." Generally, I'm never late by more than a week. Besides, late birthday greetings have become my signature and an inside joke among my children.

My children and grandchildren, however, prefer to deliver their cards in person if they can. They like to see my reaction to the cards they've selected, especially the funny ones. Those make me laugh, while the sentimental ones make me cry.

Just the other day, a week before Valentine's Day, I had a very special and mysterious delivery of a series of cards during a visit with my youngest granddaughter, Cameron. She had stopped by for her weekly visit.

I swear she's 7 going on 27. I've never met anyone like her. The things she says are very wise and mature for her age. Her sense of humor is that of an observational comedian commenting on the obvious in a way that always gives me pause and makes me chuckle.

During our conversation, she held up her hand and claimed to hear a knock on the door. She jumped up and went to the door and retrieved a card with my name — "Louise" on it.

She handed it to me. I opened it and read: "Happy Valentine's Day from your secret admirer."

Cameron was excited and teased me about having a secret admirer. And I told her I never had a secret admirer except for my husband, her "papa." And there was nothing secretive about him. He always wore his heart on his sleeve.

Two Valentine's Days have come and gone since my not-so-secret admirer passed away, two years since I last received a box of chocolate-covered cherries and a Valentine signed: Love, JB. So, I was surprised by the card and the effort. But I wrote it off as a gesture from one of my sons.

Cameron was also very close to her grandfather, "papa," who always left a big impression on people that extends beyond his life. And since he's no longer here, and she likes to keep him close, she always asks questions about him.

"Nonna, what did you used to call papa?" she asked as we sat on the couch.

"Well, sometimes I called him Seamus if he was being funny, and sometimes I called him Goofy Jimmy if he was being silly. But my favorite name for him was always JB."

Soon there was a second "knock" on the door. Did I mention that my granddaughter's superpower is infra-sound hearing or the ability to hear sounds below the normal hearing range?

She was back in a flash with a second card from my secret admirer in her hand. She was quite impressed with the fact that I now had two cards. And she speculated on whether there were possibly two secret admirers. There was no way she could tell.

Shortly thereafter she excused herself so she could cross the complex to go and visit her great aunt, Ann, my sister-in-law. She hadn't been gone long before she returned to have some pasta and meatballs. She paused in between bites to announce yet a third knock on the door.

She promptly returned with a third card that read: "Dear Louise, Happy Valentine's Day from your not-so-secret admirer. Love, JB."

I had to wonder. Was Cameron the author or the just the messenger? Did her superpower enable her to hear someone whispering to her and telling her what to do?

I'd like to think so. And JB if you're listening — PS. I love you.

O Holy Night

My husband Jimmy always liked to brag about the fact that he'd been an altar boy. He particularly liked to tease his brothers, Frank and John. He'd say, "He was all saint, and they were sinners." However, anyone who ever knew Jimmy, knew that the angelic smile, curly hair, and blue eyes were the perfect cover for the little devil that he was.

Only God knew for sure just how naughty he was because he had a habit of going to St. Patrick's on Bridge Avenue to confess his sins to a deaf priest. Jimmy always got the standard three Hail Marys for his penance. "No harm, no foul," he would say, meaning that a small transgression wasn't worth punishment if no actual harm had transpired.

So, helping himself to the occasional slice of cherry pie, as it cooled on the back porch of Biley's Bakery, wasn't as bad as eating the whole pie. Many years later, my three sons would adopt the same sort of reasoning.

When the altar boy grew up, he attended the 8:30 a.m. mass at Our Lady of Mount Carmel: the "fast mass" as it was known. The Father there skipped the homily, sped through the liturgy and, because there was no music, you were out the door in 25 minutes.

A quick exit was all well and good, but I knew Jimmy missed the music. You see, he had been a choir boy and had a beautiful voice. At least that's what he told his children and grandchildren. And when he wasn't singing silly songs, he did have a nice voice.

He would even serenade me on occasion when we first started dating. In fact, Jimmy's voice was so good that in grade school, the organist asked him to sing *O Holy Night* as a solo. He was excited, embarrassed, and scared stiff. He worried about what the neighborhood boys would say when he got up to sing, or worse, what his brothers would say? He backed out at the very last minute. It was a decision he regretted his whole life. "What if?" How many times have we all said that?

Every Christmas season, when that song came on the radio, or he'd hear it in church, he'd become wistful and wishful. For Jimmy, it was valuable lesson, and one he passed on to his children. Every Christmas, he would remind his children that it's the things that you don't do that you end up regretting.

'Twas the Night Before Christmas...

When our kids were young, my husband Jimmy always read 'Twas the Night Before Christmas by Clement Clarke Moore, on Christmas Eve, hyping up the anticipation of the Christmas Day chaos that was to come.

I'd like to think that when Christmas comes around every year, many children will go to sleep with "visions of sugar plums dancing in their heads;" however, experience tells me that children will be restless in slumber dreaming about a long list of expensive and exotic toys that will push their parents over the brink into a dark landscape of anxiety and debt.

This is not a judgement by any means. It's just an observation on how times have changed. Today, money and material things have replaced the spirit of the season. Now where have you heard that before?

Jimmy also added his own special twist to the famous poem, shaping it to meet our situation at the time. In those days, Christmas was somewhat of a "lean" holiday for our kids. Presents included new pajamas and one "big" present. Sometimes it wasn't the exact toy or musical instrument on their list but a close substitute that didn't cost as much. Between me, Jimmy, and my mom, we always managed to put something under the tree.

One Christmas, to make our children feel better about our situation at the time, Jimmy told them that Mr. Moore didn't have any money to buy his children presents. But he wrote this beautiful poem for them. I'm quite sure that Professor Moore's children had plenty of Christmas presents, but that was beside the point. Jimmy never let details get in the way of a good story.

His version of how the poem came into being made them feel worse. Our kids, a sensitive lot by nature and nurture, shed big silent tears for those poor children that didn't have presents for Christmas. It prompted them to propose that perhaps they would be better off giving their own presents away to those less fortunate. It was what sociologists sometimes refer to as the "law of unintended consequences."

Jimmy convinced them that giving up their presents was a temporary solution to a bigger problem. Christmas, he explained, was not a one-day affair. Instead, goodness and kindness should be an everyday gift we give to others.

Jimmy's gift to our children that Christmas was the gift of empathy.

Over the years as our situation improved and our children got older, Jimmy no longer read the poem. Instead, he shared his own childhood Christmas memories. He told them one year that, for his family, there was no Christmas tree and no Christmas presents: only a candelabra of three electric candles in the front window. But being a family of six children, they always knew they had each other. More tears ensued as my children began to question why we celebrated such a sad season. It made Lent look positively festive by comparison.

Jimmy's gift to our children that year was the importance of being together.

There's a line in the song, "Have Yourself a Merry Little Christmas" that sums it up beautifully, "Through the years we all will be together, if the fates allow." And we've been lucky that fate and faith have been very good to us.

Jimmy's gift to our children that Christmas was that it's not the gift that matters; it's the thought that counts.

*

It's Not What
You Know...

My kids recently explained the theory of six degrees of separation to me. Of course, this concept existed in Cleveland long before they came up with a clever name for it.

Cleveland is a "small town" city, so chances are whether you're an East Sider or a West Sider, there is someone that connects you. If you grew up on the West Side, and were either Irish or Italian and Catholic, chances are it's two degrees of separation.

According to my children, this was both a blessing and a curse. Coming from such a large and extended family, everyone knew who you were. That was often enough to get you a job or a reference on a college application. On the other hand, woe betide you should you misbehave in any way because it didn't take long before word got back to family and friends.

The adage, it's not what you know but who you know that counts, is true in so many ways. And of course, it's not limited to Cleveland.

I recall the story of a friend from Youngstown who went shopping for a pinball machine for his kids. Having tried out a few machines, he finally decided on the perfect model. He looked at the price tag and asked the salesman if that was his best price.

The salesman looked him up and down and asked, "Who do you know?"

The Art of Shopping

The old saying, "the more things change, the more they stay the same," is true. Just look at shopping. It wasn't that long ago that fresh milk and eggs were delivered to your door or milk chute each day, all year long, and fresh fruit and vegetable sellers rolled their wagons down the street in the summer. Even "junk food" like pretzels and chips were delivered in large refillable tins to your door.

As the mother of seven children, I shudder to think where I would have been without a diaper service. Good old West End Diaper picked up dirty diapers and returned with bundles of clean ones wrapped in blue paper every week.

We also had loyalty programs. The king of loyalty programs was the S&H Green Stamp Program. These green stamps were available from various retailers and coincided with the amount of your purchase at the store. One book was equal to three dollars. In those days, three dollars went far. And I was always happy to fill a book or receive one as a gift from one of my aunts.

I remember taking them to the store for redemption where the cashier carefully inspected each page to make sure they were completely full and no stamps were missing. It was very exciting, whereas these days the accumulation of "points" for free merchandise has all the excitement of Internet banking.

Today, there's no romance, no anticipation, no way to physically experience that high you get from reaching a goal. Plus, there are so many programs, you lose track of them. I have more plastic tags with bar codes on my key chain than I have keys. Many of these are linked to credit cards and debit cards I don't even use.

It seems that cash is slowly becoming a thing of the past. My children have been telling me about Bitcoin, this new form of currency backed by... well, nobody's quite sure what is backing it up. I personally think it's just another form of digital dust.

Obtaining credit was also much easier when I was young. You went to the local store and you put items on your account. Your parents went to the store every Friday (payday) and paid off the account. And so it went, week in and week out. And it was interest free.

Often, when times were tough, the local store extended credit for an extra week. Everyone was good for it. That was back in the day when your reputation was priceless and paying your debts or keeping your word guaranteed that reputation. A bad reputation was a thing to be avoided at all costs.

Lately, having seen so many "reality shows," it seems to me that a bad reputation has now become a badge of honor when, in fact, a reputation is the one thing you can't buy or acquire by points. You earn it. And for my money, that's the most satisfying acquisition of all.

Don't Tell Your Father

My husband had a few house rules when our children were young: No piercings, (other than earrings for the girls), no tattoos, and no foreign steel parked in his driveway. You bought American or nothing. Those rules were in effect until you were 18 years old and able to support yourself.

By and large our children respected those rules. But our eldest son Jimmy cut it a bit close one year just three months before his 18th birthday. He and a friend decided to attend the Kentucky Derby. And in a moment of what I can only attribute to temporary insanity, he decided to get a tattoo of a beautiful three-mast schooner with a scroll beneath it that read: *Homeward Bound.*

Jimmy was a homebody who never lived more than a block away from us his entire life. So, it made sense that those words became his personal motto. But it was more than that. I suspect he felt a deep connection to the Simon & Garfunkel song of the same title, "Homeward Bound."

When he returned home from the Derby, good Catholic guilt kicked in, and he confessed his transgression to me, to his grandmother, and to his siblings. We formed a small conspiracy to protect his secret until his 18th birthday in August. It also helped that he was an apprentice cement finisher and had a steady income, thereby meeting my husband's two requirements, i.e., legal age and an income.

Unfortunately for Jimmy it was a very hot summer that year. He wore long-sleeved flannel work shirts around the house, exited the shower with two towels — one around his waist and the other around his shoulders like a shawl — and he tried not to cross paths with his father, by either working late or leaving the house early. He paid his younger siblings two dollars to act as lookouts for the arrival or departure of his father.

Meanwhile, my husband blissfully went about his day watching the comings and goings of his brood. When he wasn't working, he spent time with the family, played catch in the driveway, read the newspaper, attended wakes, and watched TV.

After a long hot summer, the big day finally arrived. We celebrated Jimmy's birthday with the traditional banana nut sheet cake from Lawson's. We used the same single red taper candle for all birthdays. We sang, Jimmy blew out the candle and wished to tell his father something.

He announced to his father that he had gotten a tattoo for his birthday. Right on cue, his siblings feigned surprise. The little ones especially had been practicing their "surprise expression" for days. We all held our breath.

My husband nodded and finished eating his cake.

My son was surprised. "You mean you're not upset?"

"Initially, I was upset, but watching you sweat all summer trying to hide it more than made up for the deception. And you didn't get it for your birthday. So go to confession for that lie!"

"How did you know?" Jimmy asked.

"Easy," his father replied. "You broke the first rule of secret keeping."

"And that is?"

"You tell one person; you tell the world." And he pointed to everyone in the kitchen.

Suddenly the kitchen emptied. The children ran out like rats deserting a sinking ship (or in this case a three-mast schooner).

✖

Sometimes You Just Have to Show Up

My son Jimmy recently shared a story with me that reflected the atmosphere and the laid-back character of our neighborhood.

My mother's favorite saying was, "And this too shall pass." And of course, she was right. My best friend, Palma, would shrug her shoulders and say, "Whattya gonna do?" Ah those collective words of wisdom.

Two of my seven children inherited the "laid-back gene" while the other five are as high strung as their Irish father. Perhaps it's genetic. "Whattya gonna do?"

But back to Jimmy's story. He did everything last minute, at the eleventh hour and/or just in the nick of time. Homework was completed on the bus; he'd be buttoning up his cassock and straightening his surplus as he dashed onto the altar to serve Mass. And finally, he nearly delayed my daughter's wedding because he was laying off a few bets at the racetrack with his brothers just before the Mass.

His friends were a lot like him. They always took things as they came. Take, for example, his friend Spike, who woke up one morning and decided that he would get his asbestos removal certification. And, as the course was due to start the following day in Youngstown, there was no time to plan.

Lack of a plan combined with lack of a car meant that poor Spike would miss his opportunity. Unless he could find somebody who had a car and no plans, to drive him to the Avalon Hotel in Youngstown.

Finding a willing driver with no plans amongst my son's friends wasn't difficult. What was difficult was inducing them to make the one-and-a-half-hour drive. His friends always worried that something better might come up.

Number one on the list of drivers was Spike's cousin, Bengie, who had a car but no desire to visit Youngstown unless there was a valid reason. It turns out the valid reason was within the pages of Bengie's coupon book. Bengie always loved a good deal, and there was a deal to be had in Youngstown. "Buy one dozen donuts and get the second dozen free." Spike was nearly there. All he had to do was to find Bengie a co-pilot.

That co-pilot turned out to be Jimmy. Upon arriving at the hotel, they discovered that both the hotel and the course were full and there was no space available. Naturally.

Youngstown has been a hard luck town for years. The hotel clerk, who knew a thing or two about what having a job means to a young man, offered Spike a cot in the ballroom provided he got up and ready before the attendees arrived. He also squeezed Spike onto the enrollment list. It was as easy as that.

I commented to Jimmy that Spike was very lucky indeed to have made it to Youngstown and into the program. Jimmy agreed and said that sometimes luck is only half of it. The other half of it is showing up. How many people don't show up and then curse their luck?

When I asked Jimmy how Spike made it back home after he and Bengie left, he said he didn't know. Spike had no plans for the return trip. Maybe he took the bus or maybe he got a lift back with another student. Jimmy commented that Spike did what everybody in the neighborhood does, "they go with the flow." And that is the next generation's contribution to the collective wisdom of the neighborhood.

✍

Walk a Mile in Her Shoes

This is my third story about shoes. And I don't know why. Maybe it's an Italian thing? After all, Italians are famous for their footwear.

Unfortunately, all the subjects of my stories aren't lucky enough to even own a pair of Payless shoes let alone a pair of Ferragamo flats, but our family has been truly blessed over the years. So, it was no surprise when my son "donated" a pair of his father's only dress shoes to a homeless man. And then my grandson, carried on the tradition by doing the same thing in a slightly different fashion.

This story comes to me by way of a family friend. And although it sounds somewhat like a fairy tale or an urban myth, it's true. And, like all fairy tales, it starts out rather grim. It's about a homeless woman who was roaming the streets of Gotham practically barefoot. The way it was described to me, she sounded just like the poor soul in Phil Collins's song, "Another Day in Paradise." It talks about a woman who has been trying to walk but can't because she has blisters on the souls of her feet.

In the real version of this story, that is true. But instead of asking for help from the passersby on the street, she wandered into a doctor's office. The receptionist and the nurse tried to shoo the poor woman away before she could scare off the well-heeled patients sitting in the waiting room.

The doctor, hearing the commotion, left his examining room to see what was going on and sized up the situation in an instant. And because he was a compassionate man, he escorted the woman into

the examining room where he did his best to get her back on her
feet, including giving her some money to buy some new shoes. He
told her to come back in five days so he could check her feet.

Some weeks passed, and he occasionally thought about this woman and whether she purchased the shoes she so desperately needed.
He kept an eye out on the street for her but he never saw her again.

Months later, he received a call from a lawyer, asking him if he was
the doctor who had treated one of his firm's clients. The doctor didn't
recognize the name and said "no." However the lawyer continued and
described his client, who just happened to be the homeless woman.

The doctor asked about her, only to learn that she had passed
away recently. The doctor was sorry to hear that. And then he asked
the lawyer if there was anything he could do? The lawyer said "yes,
there was something the doctor could do." He asked the doctor if he
would be so kind as to meet with him to sign some papers.

You see, the old woman had left him a brownstone in her will. And
that's what happens when you put yourself in someone else's shoes.

ϑ

The Sixth Sense

Depending on your perspective, I have been either blessed or cursed with the ability to sense things. Déjà vu, vibes, dreams are all a part of my daily existence. It's not always easy to feel these things but I've gotten used to it.

I believe we all have an ability to sense things. Animals have a great sixth sense; you see them reacting to events like natural disasters hours before we humans become aware of what's happening. I also see it in children. Imaginary friends? They may be imaginary to you.

Just because you can't see things with your eyes doesn't make them any less real. I often think of what Hamlet said to his friend Horatio. "There are more things in heaven and earth, Horatio, then is dreamt of in your philosophy."

And that is how I explained a recent experience I had to my granddaughter, Bridget, who is a nurse. And, as a nurse, she is highly scientific in her analysis of physical phenomena. However, she knows that even in medicine there are a lot of things that lack explanation. And, as a woman of great faith, she knows that miracles happen every day, so my communing with the spirits on a regular basis is more normal than paranormal to her.

Recently we took a drive back to the old neighborhood for a little visit. As we walked around the streets, it was nice to relive some old memories with her. I showed her where I grew up and where her grandfather used to live. Most of the houses in the neighborhood were still there.

What had changed, though, were all the shops that lined Detroit Avenue between West 69th and West 65th. The storefronts looked so different to me now; I was only able to identify a handful of places. And that made me a little sad.

To cheer me up, Bridget took me into an ice cream shop called Sweet Moses. It was a charming place that harkened back to the days of real soda shops where ice cream was prepared and served by soda jerks. Yes, that's a real term!

Sitting there, I was overcome with a sense of nostalgia. How many soda counters had I sat at during my youth? But that wasn't all. Sitting there I felt a warm sensation surround me. I asked Bridget if the heat was perhaps up too high. But she felt no such thing.

And then it hit me, as I looked around the shop, I recognized it. It came zooming at me like a blast from the past. This wasn't really a soda shop; it had once been my Aunt Justina's tailor shop and dry cleaner. And that's when I realized that warm feeling surrounding me felt just like a hug, a hug, that my aunt gave me whenever I would visit her shop. Holy Moses!

✍

God Only Knows... and He's Not Telling

make lots of trips to the neighborhood, especially during Lent. I go to Mass, the Stations of the Cross, or just to reflect.

On a recent trip, I had exited off I-71 and Denison Avenue. And, as usual, I caught the red light. And that light has got to be the longest light in the city. Ah, I thought, it's a good test of my patience during Lent.

As I sat there, I noticed a scruffy, young, homeless man standing on the median with a sign that said, "I'm Hungry." I'm as guilty as the next person for thinking "Why doesn't' he get a job?"

It's not the most charitable thought to have had on the way to church now, is it? I wondered next what kind of cross he was carrying. It's easy to see Christ's cross in a church but not so easy to see that cross or Christ in others. Overcome with shame and guilt, I rolled down my window and handed him two dollars.

By then the light had changed and the cars behind me were becoming impatient. "Move it, lady!" cried one driver. I was tempted to yell back, "Would you blow your horn at God and tell Him to move it? This poor young man could be God in disguise." But I didn't.

That driver's behavior is between him and God. And God help him!

No Guts/
No Glory!

My late husband used to wear his heart on his sleeve but kept his colors — green, white, and orange — close to his heart. Sure, he was an Irishman through and through, and although he did celebrate St. Patrick's Day as a young man, as he grew older and wiser he took a more sober approach.

Nothing pleased him more than a good party among friends and family. And the best-loved, best-attended party on the West Side was at the McNamara's. Year in and year out, in a little house that seemed to have elastic walls, the "Macs" played host to hundreds of people of all ages, including some of Cleveland's finest first responders.

In 2015, due to illness, Jimmy couldn't attend the party but he called the house, and they played the bag pipes for him over the phone. It really lifted his spirits.

At every party, children would scamper among the adults, the old Irish immigrants would sing rebel songs, and those who knew how to step dance would do a jig or a reel. And even those who didn't at least tried. Strangers were made welcome as is the Irish custom, and old friends caught up.

Steaming trays of corned beef and cabbage rolled out of the kitchen as if on an assembly line. The beer flowed like a fountain. And the drink of choice was always Pabst Blue Ribbon, a tradition that started before we had Great Lakes. For the designated drivers, there was Barry's or Lyon's tea and scones. The term "falling down drunk" would never apply because there were so many people standing shoulder to shoulder there was no opportunity to sit down let alone fall down.

Everyone drank his fill and then some. And soon the night wore into day, and breakfast was served. The house was put in order and reset for a second round of festivities the next day. Yes, that's correct: a second party called the Guts Party. As the Macs like to say, if you have the guts to show up again and pick up where you left off, then you are welcome!

Here's Céad Míle Fáilte *to friend and to rover*
That's a greeting that's Irish as Irish can be
It means you are welcome
A thousand times over
Wherever you come from.
Whosoever you be.

Happy St. Patrick's Day to all the Macs, to Eamon Moran, my favorite Irishman after Jimmy, and all the Westside Irish. Up Mayo!

Child's Play

S ome people are lucky enough to retain a childlike sense of play their entire lives. And the person who embodied that most in our family was my husband, Jimmy. He was just a big kid at heart who enjoyed the company of his children, the neighborhood kids, and his nieces and nephews.

Whether he was teaching them how to ride a bike down our gravel driveway, playing catch in the backyard, or acting as official kickball pitcher, he always tried to instill teamwork, good sportsmanship, and a sense of fun in these activities.

Sometimes he was silly, and many times he wouldn't quite play fair. But as he used to tell me, "Life isn't always fair." Take, for example, the summer of the banana splits. Back in the day, we used to treat all the kids to a soft custard cone from the ice cream shop at the top of the street. At ten cents a cone, we could afford to treat our children and the neighborhood kids.

One summer, Jimmy took it into his head to offer everyone a banana split if each one could catch the softball he'd throw to them. That was a big IF. It took all summer before all the kids figured out his wily ways. Every night after supper they all lined up in the backyard. Each one punched his or her baseball glove rhythmically in anticipation, eyeing Jimmy warily. What was he going to do now they wondered?

He was a tricky one that Jimmy. If they scanned the trees for a pop-up fly, he threw it at their knees. If they prepared for a fast ball, he threw a sinker or curve ball. It took all summer, but they finally did it. They finally figured it out. One hot summer night every single one of them finally caught whatever Jimmy could throw at them, even my five-year-old son Michael.

That was it. Jimmy was on the hook for eight banana splits. And at 0.75 cents a piece that was quite a chunk of change for us to absorb. I was scrambling for loose change to try and cover Jimmy's extravagant prize.

Jimmy of course was unfazed by the whole thing. He calmly marched the entire troop into the kitchen. Hot and sweaty, their dirt-streaked faces bore witness to their herculean efforts as they waited for Jimmy to grab his wallet and pay up.

Jimmy did pay up but not in the way they expected. That was one thing you could always count on with him. Expect the unexpected. (More about that later). He reached on top of the refrigerator and pulled down a bunch of bananas. What he did next stunned his young charges. He promptly took a banana and cut it in half for each of them, splitting one each between the players.

Cries of "Not fair! Not fair!" rang out through the kitchen.

"How so," Jimmy wanted to know? "Isn't this a banana split?"

Jimmy turned the experience into a teachable moment quoting the immortal Yogi Berra.

"Kids," he said. "Remember that 'baseball is ninety percent physical. The other half is mental.'"

They'd been tricked by a sly fox, and they knew it. "Do over!" they yelled.

And "do over" they did but not before clearly outlining the terms and conditions of the prize. This time it had to be a real banana split, with three scoops of ice cream, toppings, nuts, and whipped cream. And it had to be served in a plastic banana boat. And it had to be purchased at the custard store at the top of the street.

"Done!" said Jimmy.

Lucky for me, it took another two weeks before they were all able to catch the softball. During that time I was able to find enough loose change to cover the cost of more prizes. One thing for sure, child's play in our family was certainly enough to keep me busy!

You'll Never Walk Alone

April has always been the hardest month for me. It's the end of winter and the beginning of spring. I find it ironic that over the years, in the month of rebirth, I've lost three of the people who were dearest to me: my mom, and my brothers Carmen and Tony. I was well and truly an orphan and the young me — the Louisa of the old neighborhood — was alone.

My husband Jimmy always knew this was a bad month for me and held his breath and my hand until the "sad season" passed. He was so conscious of my struggle that even when he was sick and dying at the end of April 2015 he hung on until May 1st before he decided to go home to God. And even though I was surrounded by loving family and friends, I felt even more alone.

Since then, my family has always made sure that April was a busy month. With the help of my daughter, I started a blog in April 2016 where I first began to write my stories of the neighborhood. Then I acquired my beloved dog Luigi in April 2017. In 2018, I took a bus trip with my in-laws to a casino in Toledo. I know that my mom, brothers, and Jimmy would have approved.

On the bus ride, Eamon, a family member by marriage, pulled me aside. "I have something for you," he said.

"Is it money?" I joked.

It turned out to be even better. He took my hand placed a beautiful rosary in it. He told me that my mother had given him that rosary 40 years earlier when she returned from a visit to Rome. I'd no idea. And now he wanted me to have it.

I was pleased and surprised and, of course, insisted that he keep it because mom had given it to him. But he persisted. And so, I put it in my purse. I thought perhaps it would bring me luck. Little did I know that later that night it would bring me something much better than luck.

After my gambling paid for another chandelier at the casino, we made the long bus trip home. Once home, I had a light bite, put the rosary next to my mom's picture on the dresser, and then fell exhausted into bed. I was just on the edge of sleep when I felt someone looking at me. I thought perhaps granddaughter had come in to check on me.

I opened one eye and waved her away. I was fine. But the figure didn't budge. I opened both eyes and saw the flickering figure of my mother standing at the foot of my bed. And then I knew.

At that moment, even though all those people that I loved were no longer with me, I wasn't alone. My mother came back to remind me that we are body and soul. And although the body may be gone, the soul is eternal. She'd showed up just when I needed her most. And her message to me is to always remember you'll never walk alone.

Off to the Zoo

M y husband Jimmy was known to tell a tall tale or two. He didn't quite lie so much as stretch the truth. I was reminded of that recently when I happened to be going through a box of old photographs.

One Sunday, he volunteered to take the three youngest children, then six, five and three years old to the zoo. I thought that was wonderful because it gave me an afternoon off and would be a learning experience for the children. I was a bit concerned about how he would manage the three of them on his own, but he reassured me everything would be fine. And so off they went to the zoo — at least that's what he told me!

Jimmy was pleased with himself when he returned. The kids said they'd had a good time and that they liked the animals. And I was none the wiser. That is, until a large brown envelope arrived in the mail a week later. It was a photo from the racetrack. It was a souvenir of the horse, jockey, and the owner and his friends in the winner's circle.

Jimmy had a wide circle of friends, one of whom was the horse's owner, so it was no surprise that he and the kids were invited to be part of the group shot. What was a surprise to him was that the picture was mailed to our house addressed to our family.

When he came home from work, I asked him about his recent trip to the zoo as I placed the photo in front of him, and he calmly explained that the racetrack was just like the zoo. After all, both places had animals. And the children got to pet them.

Our Lady of the Neighborhood

I n the Catholic Church, there seems to be as many names for Mary as there are days in the year. For example, there's Our Lady of Good Help, Our Lady of Consolation and, of course, Our Lady of Mount Carmel, which is the name of our parish church and school. But I prefer to think of her as Our Lady of the Neighborhood because she was always there watching over us.

When I think back on it, there were lots of examples of how Our Lady interceded daily for her many children. I like to call them everyday miracles. In addition to the everyday miracles, there were times when the miracles were so incredible, we could hardly believe our eyes or ears. They were truly a result of divine intervention. In our neighborhood, there seemed to be one miracle every decade for as far back as I can remember.

The first one I remember happened when I was just five years old. As children, we often played in the street in front of our tightly packed houses. Since not many people had cars in those days, most of the traffic was limited to the semi-trailer trucks making their way to the factory at the bottom of the street.

One day, my brother Carmen who was about seven years old at the time, dashed out between two parked cars without checking for oncoming traffic. He didn't see the semi heading right for him. But my grandmother did. We all did. Powerless to do anything, she instinctively cried out for help to the Mother of God: "Santa Maria! Holy Mary!"

Our Lady heard her because the truck stopped within inches of my brother. His life was spared thanks to Our Lady of the Semis.

The 1940s was a time of great hardship for everyone. I'm referring to the Second World War and all the men and women we lost overseas in the fighting. Service Flags, bearing stars, hung in nearly all the windows of the neighborhood. So many men and women were killed, were prisoners of war, or just missing in action.

My husband Jimmy's cousin was one of the missing. His aunt had a rose bush on the side of the house that failed to bloom the summer her son went missing. And every year after that, while her garden was a riot of flowers, the rose bush refused to bloom. That was until the year after the war ended. That summer, much to everyone's surprise, the bush bloomed. That was the year Jim's cousin came home. That was thanks to Our Lady of the Roses.

Our son Michael was also a little miracle. He was born with a congenital heart defect that, in the 1960s, was not easily treated by surgery. In fact, there wasn't much medicine could do at the time either. But that didn't stop his Aunt Mary Catherine who, thanks to her great faith and persistence, went to Mass every morning at 6:30 where she prayed away for a miracle, which was granted by our Lady, the Queen of Hearts.

In the 1970s, a young man from the neighborhood, Jimmy C, undertook a very dangerous mission to smuggle Bibles and Catechisms into communist Romania. Jimmy was — and still is — a defender of the faith and our country's way of life. Jimmy returned home safely and was able to tell his amazing story thanks to the protection of Our Lady of the Warriors.

In the 1980s, my husband ran for public office. And he lost. And I'm not unhappy about that. His heart was in the right place, but at the end of the day he was too plain spoken to be a good politician. And just between you and me, we had Our Lady of Unanswered Prayers to thank for that one.

In the last few decades, it may have looked like all was lost and that our little Italian neighborhood was on the decline. It might have even looked like Our Lady of the Neighborhood was busy elsewhere.

But she wasn't. She was there quietly working behind the scenes. And just when you think all is lost, a rose finally blooms and there's an answer to a prayer.

✍

All Roads
Lead to Home

My niece recently said to me at a bridal shower, "Aunt Lou. I still have dreams about your house."

She meant our century-old home in Cleveland. It was a grand old house that dominated the street. It accommodated me, Jimmy, my mother, seven children, a menagerie of animals, and various family and friends who came for visits or sometimes to stay awhile. No matter how many people we had, there always seemed to be enough room.

I fell in love with that house the moment I set eyes on it. In fact, even though we weren't looking for a house, it showed up at just the right time. Jimmy and I weren't married long, and we were living outside the neighborhood. We were renting the lower half of a double. It was fine, except that it was just far enough from the neighborhood that I couldn't walk home. We had to drive.

One fine Saturday afternoon in 1964 I was waiting for Jimmy to come home so we could take the children and go and visit my mother. And wait I did. Jimmy showed up four hours late. The kids had already fallen asleep. I was not happy with him because he hadn't called, and I'd gotten worried.

He explained that he was out with his Godfather, Ray, and that they were looking at a house. It was a house he had no intention of buying. We couldn't afford it. We didn't have a down payment, and we had three children. My guess is that they were at a "public house," i.e., a local bar, having a few drinks. And, if his breath was any indication, he'd had his fair share of beer.

Playing along, I said, "I didn't know we were in the market for a house. But now that you mention it, that's a good idea."

And much to Jimmy's shock and amazement, I phoned his Godfather Ray and asked him to take me to see the house. Much to my shock and amazement there really was a house to be seen. And Ray was only happy to take me. He knew the owners and he felt that he could help us seal the deal.

And such a deal it was. The house cost $10,000. But we had one small problem: our rental agreement wasn't up for many months. And we couldn't afford both places.

As luck would have it, our landlord asked us if we could move out of the double to accommodate his newly married son who was looking for a place to live. It looked like the stars were aligning in our favor. And from that day forward, although we had our ups and downs, that house was magical and filled with memories. It withstood tornadoes, blizzards, and meteorites that Jimmy mistook for aliens when they landed in the funeral home parking lot across the street. And he was stone cold sober when he saw them. But that's another story for another time.

My son Jimmy recently reminded me of the many times our house gave shelter during some severe natural disaster. The first time was during the tornado of 1969. Our house, which was just south of Lake Erie, gave shelter to dozens of people fleeing the Lake after the July 4th fireworks. Total strangers and neighbors took shelter in our home and waited out the storm.

And, in January 1978, a blizzard covered the city, knocking out power and heat. Again, our house became a refuge for neighbors until the power came on. Our kids still refer to it as the neighborhood slumber party, the one they always wanted as kids but which we never allowed.

Occasionally, when I go to Mass in the neighborhood, I go back and visit our old house. The neighborhood has changed a lot since the days when we lived there. But there she sits atop the street, towering over the neighboring houses, like a mother hen watching her chicks.

And when I see her, because my house is a "her," I have this urge to ask the owners to rent it to me for just one night. One night where I'd have my own brood, just my children, come home and spend the night. My kids like to tease me about this. And on more than one occasion they have talked me out of knocking on the door to accost the poor unsuspecting owners.

And perhaps they're right to do that. And while it saddens me that I can't turn back the clock, I take comfort in the wise words of the Polish poet, Stanislaw Jerzy Lec, who said, "You can close your eyes to reality but not to memories."

Kids Say the Darndest Things

Years ago, there used to be a talk show program on TV hosted by Art Linkletter called *Kids Say the Darndest Things*. And that's true. You have only to talk or listen to a child to gain a fresh perspective on things.

I remember years ago, in 1976, the year of the American Bicentennial, overhearing a conversation between my youngest son Danny and his best friend, Tommy. They might have been about seven or eight years old at the time.

Danny and Tommy attended different schools. Danny went to the local Catholic school and Tommy to the local public school. In fact, that's how my children identified themselves back then. You were either Catholic or "Public" which was a catch-all term for anyone who was not Catholic.

Catholicism colored their everyday lives. Take, for example, the different perspectives shared by the two boys on a fine summer's day.

Danny pointed to the sky as a large white bird landed on the garage roof.

"Look, Tom!" he said, "It's the Holy Spirit!"

"No, it's not," Tommy said. "It's the Spirit of '76!"

Either way, I said, "God Bless, America!"

And God Bless, Mom!

Easy Money

According to my son, Jimmy, easy money always comes at a price. He likes to reminisce about how back in the day, when he was young and perhaps a little foolish, he was always in search of fast cash with little effort. His favorite "get-rich-quick" scheme was the Ohio lottery.

Always the optimist, he ignored the odds of one in 14 million to spend a portion of his weekly paycheck on lottery tickets. But my kids have always been lucky at games of chance, and so he blissfully ignored the odds. Why not him, he thought. Why not indeed because once, a long time ago, he came very close to winning it all — so close that to this day his heart still pounds in his chest just thinking about it.

That week he bought his ten tickets at a convenience store nearby his grandmother's apartment. As was his usual habit on a Friday night, he headed over there for dinner, a chat with Nonna, and to check his previous week's tickets, which he kept under a statue of St. Jude. (St. Jude is the patron saint of hopeless cases.)

He took the first ticket and laid it on the kitchen table and compared it to the winning numbers in the newspaper. The first number was a match. But one number means nothing. The second number was also a match. Close but no cigar. His finger running across the page, he sees that he has three numbers that match. Lucky him, he thought, that's good for a free ticket. He'd been there before.

He continued and found his fourth number was also a match. Now there was some money to be had, he figured. That could be worth about fifty dollars. Still, six matching numbers was impossible, or so he thought until he found the fifth match. Even if he didn't get all six numbers, five winning numbers would be a substantial amount of money.

He was afraid to continue. At that point he got up from the kitchen table and walked out on to the balcony. He looked at the sun setting over Lake Erie and he prayed. "God," he said, "if I win this money, I promise you I will do my best. And if I don't win, it doesn't matter."

He went back into the apartment and resumed his task of checking for the final lottery number. Unfortunately, he didn't have all six winning numbers. Still, a five out of six streak would pay handsomely, or so he thought.

That night he went to sleep with visions of dollar signs dancing in his head. Sure, he'd have to keep his day job, but in the meantime, he could do some shopping. He bought me a new refrigerator, four new tires for his car, and took his girlfriend out to a fancy restaurant for dinner. All totaled, he must have spent $1200.00 of his newfound winnings.

In his excitement, he never bothered to check the actual payout. He didn't count on sharing the pot with several hundred other lucky winners. His luck had run out. He won only $400.00. That meant there was a big deficit he'd have to make up.

He was back to making money the old-fashioned way: he had to earn it.

The House Everyone Called Home, Part 1

We raised our seven children in a house that was built in 1900. It was the biggest house on the street. And to this day, my children's friends always remember it as the biggest, busiest, and best house on the street.

We had seven children and counting... if you included all the friends, nieces and nephews. My husband used to say, "as long as I count seven heads in the bed at night, we're good." He was not a detail person. But I always made sure they were the right heads.

The backyard had a garage, a basketball court, and a path that served as a cut through to the next street. Some of the kids that cut through our backyard we knew and others we did not. But everyone was respectful.

My sons always left the basketball out underneath the rim so that anyone passing through could take a shot if they wanted. Everyone, even the strangers, knew the rules. Take the basketball with you and there would be no replacement. We never lost that ball.

The other rule was, if you're playing in the backyard, you did "garage door duty" every time our neighbor Nanny came home from church or shopping. We had a shared driveway and Nanny always got valet service when she pulled up to her garage. There was no such thing as an electric garage door opener in those days. You had to manually open and shut the garage door. Again, that was another rule that was never broken.

By all appearances it was a busy yard especially in summer, with kids riding their bikes in and out, playing kickball in the street, throwing around a baseball and climbing trees. And then one day it all stopped. There wasn't a kid to be found anywhere.

I was suspicious. I took a walk to the backyard. And as I approached the garage, it sounded like there was a party going on inside. Shouting and laughing and cheering.

I pushed open the door, and what did I see? The garage was converted into a casino with a huge gaming wheel made of cardboard, and a betting table with numbers. Above the table, a sign read: The Big Six. My youngest son Danny was running a small business with the help of his two older brothers, Jimmy and Michael.

I cleared the premises. Now I knew how Jesus felt clearing the temple. The neighborhood kids left in a hurry.

"Couldn't you open a lemonade stand?" I yelled. And then I added for good measure, "You're all grounded!" And that includes you too," I said and pointed to the few remaining kids that were brave enough to wait to collect their winnings.

My sons protested, "But we saw a wheel just like it at the Feast!"

They did have a point there. As I marched my boys into the house it occurred to me. Why should I punish myself? Having those three in the house together on a hot summer day was probably not a good idea. I changed my tack and decided to send them back out instead.

But not before they apologized, promised they wouldn't do it again, and agreed to clean the garage out from top to bottom, starting with the casino. They were as good as their word, and with my sons you could always bet on that!

*

The House Everyone Called Home, Part 2

Our house was always the gathering point for all the kids in the neighborhood. Looking back on it, I could have opened my own school.

We were like Grand Central Station, providing forgotten lunches, last-minute homework assignments, Band-Aids, and hair braids, as well as an occasional wipe with the *mappine** across a dirty face. However, for as much as we gave, we always received equal measure in return.

All I can say was thank goodness for all those extra children who appeared on our doorstep every morning as regular as clockwork. They were better than clocks. I owe more than one of them a huge debt of gratitude for keeping my children off the tardy list. I especially owe my adopted daughter, Patrizia, big time.

There was more than one occasion when we would all oversleep only to be roused by banging on the front door. It was Patrizia. "Get up! Get up! We're going to be late for Mass." And by "we," she always included herself in that group because she would never leave without my oldest daughter and the rest of the kids in tow.

Oh, and lest I forget, where there are kids there's usually a dog. And our family dog, Pete, was always one to tag along with the group. In fact, Pete was also known to attend both Mass and school. It wasn't unusual for me to get a call from the local priest or nuns at the school. "Louisa, come and get Pete, he's in school again." Or, "Louisa, come and get Pete, he's in church again."

I'm betting Pete was probably St. Francis of Assisi in another life, except that he could sometimes be mysterious and disappear for days. I suspect he had a girlfriend in the next block. Sometimes he would be gone for weeks. But he would always come home. He had instinctual radar for that big house and all those kids. My kids have that same radar and so do their friends; they show up on my doorstep in the suburbs on a regular basis. Just like Pete, they still know how to find home.

Special note here — as we are southern Italians, we have a habit of dropping the last vowel on most words. The proper word is mappina and that means dish towel.

Grand Central Station... West 73rd

By my son, Michael

D id you know a train arrives at New York's Grand Central Station terminal every 58 seconds during the morning rush hour? Well, during the school year we had our own version of Grand Central Station. Instead of trains, we had kids stopping by every three minutes to meet up with my brothers and sisters to make the trek to our grade school, Our Lady of Mount Carmel.

Our house was centrally located, so it was the perfect spot for all our friends living north of Herman Avenue and west of our house between 74th and 85th streets. During those cold Cleveland winters, when the Canadian north winds blew off the lake, or in spring, when a thunderstorm popped up unexpectedly, Grand Central Station West 73rd provided temporary safe harbor.

All tracks led to our front door, and my mother was the perfect conductor. She ran the day's schedule with the precision of a Swiss watch. She ensured that forgotten lunches were quickly made up in the kitchen and missing hats, gloves, and scarves were doled out to whoever needed them.

In the case of forgotten homework, she made a quick phone call and delivered it personally to an anxious student. On the flip side, there were times where our friends would remind us of something we needed, like gym clothes, permission slips, or after-school practice schedules.

The "platform" where all this took place was the vestibule at our front door. I call it a vestibule, but it was more like an anteroom that could hold up to six kids at one time. It held everything we needed for those cold Cleveland winters. Our coats were heaped on top of a freestanding coat rack with little attention given to size, season, or owner. Finding and removing your coat was like playing a life-sized game of Jenga every day. Remove the wrong coat and you risked the entire rack falling on top of you.

It was a daily game of strategy and nerve, as my brother Danny can attest to. One winter morning, we found the coat rack on the floor, the coats in a heap and Danny buried underneath the pile. Luckily my grandmother noticed a small pair of boots poking out from under the coats; otherwise, he might have missed school that day. (Actually! I think that was his plan all along). You can imagine what kind of note my mother would have had to write. "Instead of catching a cold he literally caught coats."

Since there were seven of us in school at that time — and with friends arriving every few minutes — there was bound to be overcrowding. The kids would spill over into the living room. My father, who oversaw crowd control, did his best to try and keep my mother's new shag carpet dry. But it was impossible. Once everybody shuffled into the house, my dad had two rules: the girls had to sit, and the boys had to take off their hats while in the house. No exceptions! If you could not abide by those rules, you waited on the porch.

The daily ritual we had of coming together cemented friendships we carry with us to this day. The friends we made were, and are still, our companions on life's long (and sometimes too short) road. Thinking back on all those kids, picturing them in my mind, I felt a little bit like Romper Room's Miss Barbara looking through her magic mirror to see: Patty, Gina, Kenny, Gino, Michael, Susie, Stacy, Ritchie, Carl, Gary, David, Roger, Tony, Sissy, Shelly, and Shannon.

∽

Teach Your Children Well

My husband came from a large Irish family with three sisters and two brothers. When you add up all the children in the next generation, there are 28 first cousins: "The Cousins" as they like to call themselves.

They are a clannish lot; there isn't a baptism, first communion, confirmation, graduation, family picnic, or wedding that doesn't involve them, and that includes the grand openings of several pubs on Cleveland's West Side. The Cousins could make or break any social event either by attending or not. To see them walk into to a function all together was a sight to behold.

They're all grown up now, with children and grandchildren of their own but, despite their busy schedules, they still manage to get together and to stick together. My daughter Margaret marvels at the fact that in a day and age where people constantly move and relocate to places far away, nearly all of them have stayed within short drives of their parents. Only three of The Cousins live out of town. And they make regular visits home, like swallows going back to Capistrano. And when they get home, in the words of the Blues Brothers, the "band is back together."

My oldest daughter Catherine, also the "oldest" cousin, likes to joke about the separation anxiety they used to feel as children when they listened to the stories of how their dad and his siblings were temporarily separated as children. You see, while most parents read bedtime stories about giants and princesses to their kids, my husband told his children about the tough times growing up in Cleveland in the 1940s and 1950s.

I think the story that touched them all the most was about how Jimmy, and his brothers and sisters were parceled out to relatives until their parents could get back on their feet financially. The thought of their uncle John sleeping in the back of a parked car at night, or their dad not being able to see his own sisters, reduced my children to tears.

It was the Mulgrew equivalent of the "I walked five miles to school in bare feet in the snow" lesson other parents tell their children to teach them about gratitude. It was also his way of teaching them empathy, and it worked. Sad movies, sentimental commercials, anyone in distress affects them all.

My kids and their cousins are a kindhearted lot. They are always there for family, friends, even strangers, at the drop of a hat. When I had bypass surgery thirteen years ago; the hospital waiting room was filled to overflowing with my children, my in-laws, nieces, nephews, and friends. They rotated in and out as their schedules allowed. The coffee table was laden with casseroles, salads, sandwiches, and desserts. There was enough food to feed the folks in the waiting room and the nurse's station. Our family deals with joy and stress in the same way — with food.

One nurse was so astonished by the crowd; she asked my son Michael if the patient was someone famous. Perhaps a politician? He laughed and said, "Well, she's famous to us." When he told her that this crowd was only a few family members and friends she was amazed. She'd never seen anything like it.

Years later, as I think about this, I reflect on how gratifying it is to be a part of such an amazing family. It reminds me of a line from the Crosby, Stills, Nash & Young song, "Teach Your Children Well," a song my son Michael plays on his guitar. There's one line that touches me the most, "So, just look at them and sigh, and know they love you." They also love each other.

We taught them well.

Let the Games Begin

This terrible pandemic has more and more families staying at home. For most people, it's a difficult thing to do, but also the best way to keep people safe. But there's also a need to keep people occupied or entertained. As I tell my grandchildren, you can only watch so much television and play so many video games. They didn't quite believe me and asked me what I would have done at their age to pass the time.

Well, I'm glad they asked. When I was a young girl (goodness, do I feel ancient just saying that!) we did lots of things that didn't cost a lot of money but were a whole lot of fun. I taught my children these games and they enjoyed them immensely. Of course, I had to referee the occasional dispute, but these games kept them busy for hours.

I taught them how to play pick-up sticks, jacks, tiddlywinks, and hangman. My kids had more fun saying tiddlywinks than they ever had playing it. The sound of it made them crack of up laughing.

The kids enjoyed the games and the competition of trying to best each other. Although, I did have to confiscate the wooden paddle ball so their coordination, or lack thereof, wouldn't end with tears and bruises. I do wish they would have made those elastic bands shorter!

Back in the day, we used to buy these games at the Five and Dime Store where items cost a nickel or ten cents. Today's equivalent would be The Dollar Store or Dollarama, where items cost between one and five dollars. Talk about inflation!

During the pandemic, my grandchildren haven't been able to go to the store to buy any of these games. What they do now is buy them through Amazon. When they were putting together their shopping list, I had them add a bag of marbles.

"Well, grandma, if you ever lose your marbles, we'll just buy you some new ones," they joked.

I laughed and said nothing. They were about to be schooled in the fine art of losing *their* marbles. Little did they know that grandma was a "ringer." Arthritic hands aside, I was a straight shooter from way back. Really.

In 1953, I won The Cleveland Press/Greater Cleveland Marble Championship, defeating some 38 other players. That won me a spot at the national competition in Asbury Park, New Jersey. Imagine my excitement meeting and teaching Cleveland Indian's Bill Lobe and Mel Harder the proper way to hold a shooter. And imagine my grandchildren's surprise when I walked away with all the marbles.

House Rules...

My husband Jimmy was a big kid at heart. He was the Pied Piper of the neighborhood. Our yard was always full of kids. He would organize kickball matches, referee backyard hoops, and teach kids how to ride a bike on our gravel driveway. I was the nurse on call: icing sprained ankles, dressing cuts, and picking my fair share of cinders out of kids' knees.

Jimmy was a trickster of the highest order, whether he was inventing secret signals like the woodchuck sign — which required all kids to place their hands underneath their chins and flap their fingers — or assigning nicknames for which only he knew the meaning.

Take our niece Linda, for example. She is the fourth of seven children, but Jimmy insisted on calling her "Number 6" her entire life. He christened our niece, Jackie "Boompa." No rhyme or reason: that was just Jimmy.

He was not above adding a bit of a handicap when bigger or faster kids were up against smaller ones. Some might call that cheating; he called it a head start. Take the nightly sprints down the driveway. They began at the sidewalk and ended 90 feet down the bottom of driveway where you had to touch our neighbor's garage door. (Slamming into it was more like it. Thank goodness we had such understanding neighbors!)

When my son Jimmy lined up with Claudio, the fastest kid in the neighborhood, my husband Jimmy held the hem of Claudio's tee-shirt for the split second our son needed to sprint ahead. Not that it mattered. Young Jimmy could have had a half a driveway advantage, and the talented Claudio would still have overtaken him.

My husband always tried to showcase the talents of his children. One of his favorites was a totally made-up word problem. He made up the puzzle as he went along. It was a different puzzle every time.

Our Gang: back row: Gino; middle row: Mike, Patty and Catherine;
front row: Michael, Margaret and Jimmy

He trotted it out at family functions like christenings and first communions. For example, he would call upon his oldest daughter to demonstrate her mathematical prowess, which was met by a collective eye roll from her siblings because everyone knew, as did Catherine, that numbers were not her strong suit. She would make up an answer. And whatever answer she came up with my husband Jimmy would say she was right!

They were in cahoots. And Jimmy would cheer marveling at the mathematical genius that was his daughter. Here's a recap of one such "puzzle."

Jimmy: There's a high-speed train going from Cleveland to Chicago at 100 miles per hour. Inside one car there are 53 horses. In a second car, there are 107 turtles. And in the third car there are 44 monkeys. If the train slows down to 50 miles an hour in Detroit, and 4 cats get off how, many alligators are left?

Catherine rubs her chin in concentration when, suddenly, the answer hits her: 225 she says with a smile.

Jimmy heartily applauds, and all the children look on in awe and wonder at Catherine for having calculated such a difficult problem so quickly.

Jimmy's favorite game of all was the "quiet game." The first time he tried it, he enlisted about 15 children who were at our house for a birthday party. You can imagine the noise level when you mix kids with adults and the family dog. To dial it down and give the adults a chance to relax, Jimmy marshalled all 15 children into the den and proposed the following challenge.

Whoever could be the quietest child for the longest period, he said, pointing to the clock on the mantle, would win one dollar. He laid a crisp dollar bill on top of the mantle within sight of the participants. Then he went and stood just outside the door and listened. It didn't take long for the whispering to start. When it did, he stepped back in and caught the culprits, cousins Pat and Tommy, talking. OUT! He said as he banished them to the backyard.

The rest of the children sat in stone cold silence, eyeing the dollar on the mantle. They weren't going to make the same mistake and get caught talking. A house full of children so quiet that you could hear a pin drop both surprised, and worried, the adults in the kitchen. They wondered what was going on. Jimmy reassured them that the kids were all fine, just playing a game in the den.

When it was time to award the prize, Jimmy asked the kids if anyone had talked: They all shook their heads 'no.' But my daughter, Margaret Mary, spoke up and identified nearly every kid in the room who couldn't resist temptation and had whispered — if only a little. Before long, everyone was out of the money, as was Margaret Mary for tattling.

No fair! You cheat! They would all cry as Jimmy would smile and say half-jokingly/half seriously: "Sorry kids, my house, my rules."

✿

Once Upon a Time...

This is a book of stories. And while all of them are true, some may be what my kids call "enhanced" for maximum effect. When I was a kid, we used to call it pulling your leg or exaggerating. And it was done mostly to amuse or entertain our children.

Take my husband Jimmy; to say he was prone to exaggeration is an understatement. You never knew if he was embellishing or if he was telling the truth. He used to say, the way to get away with a tall tale is to stay as close to the truth as possible.

What follows are two good examples of how parents have captivated the attention of two generations of children: mine and my children's generation.

This first story is about my cousin Dickey and his mother, my Aunt Angie. It was post-war Cleveland, and life was starting to get back to normal. Angie decided to treat her nine-year-old son, Dickey, to a movie.

They took the streetcar to downtown Cleveland to the RKO Palace Theater to see a movie. Now, back in the day, movies were not just a couple of previews and popcorn. No way! Movies, in the big theaters like the Palace, were like fine dining, with a newsreel, a movie, and then live musical entertainment.

Some of the live music included Tommy and Jimmy Dorsey, Harry James, and Glenn Miller. Cleveland native Kay Ballard was the head usherette. Imagine! (This part is true.)

Dickey can't remember what movie he saw but he'll never forget the singer. It was none other than Louis Prima! When Louis Prima walked out on stage, Dickey's mother Angie leaned down and whispered in his ear. "Louis is your uncle, and he's going to sing a song for me. Listen carefully."

And wouldn't you know it; the song he opened with was "Angelina." Angelina means little Angie in Italian. Dickey was so excited he couldn't wait to get home and tell all the neighborhood kids about his famous uncle.

I was in awe of this famous relative and asked my mother if there was anyone on our side of the family that was famous. And without missing a beat she said Steubenville native, Dean Martin, was a cousin.

Imagine! Dickey and I couldn't believe our good fortune being related to two famous people. Or so we thought. Fast forward some seventy years later, our friends and family still can't resist ribbing us about our "famous relatives."

I think my children inherited the wonderstruck gene from me. They were also held in thrall by their father's brush with celebrity.

In the 1950s, Jimmy was a private in the US Army stationed in Wiesbaden, Germany. He was in the armored division and drove a tank. My children were fascinated by all his stories but their favorite story, the one that topped them all, was the story of how, when he was sent home, they replaced him with — drumroll — the King of Rock 'N Roll, Elvis Presley!

It had to be true! The timing was perfect. Elvis arrived in Germany in 1958, the same year Jimmy came back home. The news lit up the 1970s school yard like a thousand Klieg lights on the Oscar red carpet. The whole neighborhood basked in the halo of having an almost famous dad in their midst.

After my experience with Uncle Louis Prima and Cousin Dean Martin, I didn't have the heart to tell my children anything different. As they never questioned the fact that Elvis replaced their dad in the army. Why should I burst their bubble? I mean when it comes to a "Once Upon a Time" story, what kid doesn't want a happy ending?

Saints Preserve Us!

Three months ago, I moved in with my daughter Beth and her family. She is "the planner" among my seven children; she plans everything beautifully to the 'nth' degree. She makes everything she does look so effortless. She's like the proverbial duck gliding smoothly across the pond, all the while her little feet paddle like mad below the water's surface guiding us all from one part of the pond to another without so much as a ripple.

By the time I moved in, Beth had all my things set up in the spare bedroom in a way that made me feel right at home. There was my nightstand, with all my photos and my CD player. On top of the chest of drawers there was a little shrine of all my statues: The Blessed Mother, Saint Jude, the Blessed Sacrament, and the Holy Family.

It's very comforting to have them all with me, and the continuity of faith they represent. Recently I had a close encounter of a personal kind with them. I had gone to bed and was just on the edge sleep when a white light emanating from the dresser flickered against my closed eyes. When I opened them, I saw that the statues were illuminated. I held my breath and waited. Was I going to have visitors? Was this a sign of things yet to come, — à la Charles Dickens's *A Christmas Carol*?

But then the light suddenly disappeared just as mysteriously as it had appeared. It was probably car headlights, I thought. I closed my eyes again but when the otherworldly light appeared a second time, I thought I was imagining things.

"No one is going to believe this," so I decided I had better get a witness. I was hesitant to wake my daughter but decided to do so anyway. Why not share the experience? As I entered the kitchen, I found my grandson Brendan foraging in the fridge for a midnight snack.

"Oh, I'm sorry, Grandma," he said. "I didn't mean to wake you." I assured him that he didn't wake me, and in fact, he could be of help to me in investigating a paranormal event occurring at that very moment in the bedroom.

His blue eyes grew wide at the thought. And they grew wider still when we stood in the doorway and watched the saints self-illuminate. We looked at each other and back at the dresser. He whispered, "Do you think it's okay if we turn on the lights?"

"Go ahead," I encouraged him. "I mean if the saints are going to all this trouble to create their own light, maybe they don't like the dark."

Brendan flicked on the overhead light, and as we peered across the room at the dresser we noticed that my cellphone was also there. It was the source of the light: the text messages and voice mails sending bursts of light upward onto the statues.

We nearly woke up the entire house with our laughter. "Well," I said somewhat relieved, "at least it's not God calling. I'm still here!"

To which my darling grandson replied, "That would have been a heck of a long-distance call."

✍

Wishful Thinking...

By my oldest daughter, Catherine

My Grandma Vi passed away over three decades ago, but her wit and wisdom are still with us.

My mom, my siblings, and I are the collective repository of memories, stories, and sayings. And now these stories and sayings are being handed down to the next generation of grandchildren and great-grandchildren. Grandma Vi has become a legend. Like my mother always said, "There are the 'Ten Commandments' and then there are 'Vi's Words of Wisdom.' Neglect them both at your peril."

As the oldest child, I was always in a hurry to grow up. And Grandma Vi, in her infinite wisdom, would always try to slow me down.

"What's your rush?" she would ask. "It's when you go too fast that you make mistakes." And she was right. Whether it was helping me with my math homework or ironing a school uniform. She took her time. I never saw her rush anywhere. She calmly and collectedly glided through everyday events, crises, and catastrophes. Somewhere in her playbook she drew upon the universally accepted wisdom: "This too shall pass" and, "Take your time; you're going to grow up soon enough."

As for me, having all the confidence of a firstborn, I'd pipe up and say, "Well, it can't pass quick enough!" She'd shake her head and smile at me with more indulgence and grace than I deserved.

I often wondered if she wished for the same things when she was my age. And then before I knew it, I woke up one day and realized I'd missed a lot of the present just wishing for the future. Now, I wish I had listened to her.

That might sound a little regretful but it's not. That's because she also knew a thing or two about regret. Toward the end of her life and about halfway through mine, I told her she had been right about me missing out on the present by pursuing the future. To which she replied, "If you didn't spend all that time planning your future, you wouldn't be where you are now."

She always knew just what to say. I wish I could be more like her.

So. ... What's Your Hurry?

By my son, Michael

When I was a kid, my grandmother would always say "Don't be in such a hurry to grow up!" But I was always in a hurry, especially when I watched my older brother, Jimmy, get ready to go out on a Friday night with friends, or my sister, Catherine, driving around in her Dodge Dart she named "Simba." She would always be off somewhere with friends who appeared to live hundreds of miles away when they just lived outside of our neighborhood.

They had all the freedom I thought I lacked. My other sister, Margaret, just started working at the Pick-N-Pay a grocery store on West 65th and Franklin Avenue. I was ticked off because Margaret, with whom I was closest in age, and I are a bit competitive to say the least. She had beat me again, this time to finding some freedom first.

So, there I was, 14 years old and thinking, "Man, I can't wait until I turn 16 so I can drive. I will have so much fun if I have the freedom to travel outside of our little neighborhood. I can take my buddies on joy rides through the "Valley" (Metro Parks) or go to a movie at Great Northern Mall, and finally rid myself of public transportation. No more RTA for this guy."

So, I turn 16, get a license, and I am ready to roll. I borrowed our elderly neighbor's car to take the test. That should have been a red flag right there. "Why am I taking our elderly neighbor's 1978 Chevy Nova to take this test," I thought. Suddenly it occurred to me that, with five licensed drivers and three cars (only two operational) in the family, there weren't enough cars to go around.

My long-held dream of freedom quickly vanished. I was back on the RTA to school, and no cruising with my buddies like I'd hoped. Good news! Not long after, I got a job which finally enabled me to make a down payment on that elusive used car. I also became responsible for car payments, insurance, and gas.

I turn 18. The curfew gets extended, I am an adult (according to my birth certificate), and the freedom to come and go as I please is right there. As a senior in high school, I can attend all the cool parties and come home around one or two a.m. No more midnight curfew on Friday or Saturday nights for me. I attended a few parties and stayed out late a couple of times but couldn't do that too often because I had to be up early Saturday to go to work. Good news! I undertook a little more responsibility and I learned to be accountable.

I turn 21. I walk into a bar (legally), sit down, and have a beer. I am now a true adult, capable of making adult decisions about my future. I had already been in bars since the drinking age in Ohio was 19 at the time. Sadly, it wasn't a big deal turning 21. In fact, I worked on my birthday; it was a day just like any other. It wasn't as special as I thought it would be.

Good news! I began to understand what my grandmother meant.

So, I am 55 today and have lived a blessed life. I am lucky. I have a God of my understanding, a great family, good friends, and people who I can rely on during tough times. The "fireworks" I expected with each coming-of-age activity never happened. What did happen was that each milestone taught me a lesson.

Good news! I'm still here and in good health to enjoy them all.

Sometimes I go on social media and see a lot of "memory lane" stuff. You know, people saying "remember when?" I laugh because I am sure almost every one of us has wished our lives away while reaching for milestones that really meant nothing. The "fireworks" I expected with each coming-of-age activity never happened. What did happen though was that each milestone taught me a lesson.

If I were to take a tape measure and stretch it out to 75 inches and put my finger on my age now, I would see a lot of that tape in my past. But I am in no hurry to do that. That's like driving while looking in

Courtesy of Detroit Shoreway Community Development Organization.

the rear-view mirror. No, it's better to look ahead and take in each day as it comes.

So, the good news is that I finally learned to take my grandma's advice and slow down. I guess I'm not in such a hurry after all.

My Little Vagabond

As parents, we often hope that our children will absorb at least some of our wise counsel. Sometimes what we perceive as wisdom or good advice, when followed, brings some surprising results.

One day in a fit of pique with my husband for some minor transgression, I turned to my eldest daughter and said, "Don't get married! See the world."

She was way ahead of me. When she was six years old, she was already teaching herself French with the help of her gifted cousin Chrissie and some books from the neighborhood library. Every day she poured over all the books in the Madeline series, imagining herself strolling along the water-colored streets of Paris.

It was no surprise when she packed her little red suitcase for sleepaway summer camp at the tender age of ten, where she would, essentially, be on her own. She exhibited no fear or anxiety as she hopped on the bus. I'm not even sure she waved goodbye. She was launched on a journey that continues to this day.

People not used to a life of perpetual motion marvel at her travels. Friends and siblings live vicariously through her. Other friends worry about the lack of permanence in her life, of a soft place to land. She usually finds herself, as she says, NFA or CWC which are her acronyms for No Fixed Address or Currently without Country.

Where once she was in the minority, she now finds herself in the majority. She's part of a new group of travelers called global nomads.

They crisscross the globe in search of new experiences, depleting one bank only to add to a different kind of bank: their memory banks.

I used to think that it was my admonition all those long years ago that set her a' wandering. And I sometimes feel a bit guilty. What parent doesn't? It would be a whole lot easier if children came with instruction manuals. But since they don't, you can only do your best.

My daughter assures me that, while my words made an impression, the die was already cast. And it was her grandmother who had inoculated her against loss — the loss of place, people, or possessions — by telling her, "All you need is a place to hang your hat." And "An address is only a number."

Many years later, a friend and fellow traveler told her over lunch at a seaside tavern in Piraeus, "Home is where friends like you are." And so, for that brief instant, she was home.

Last but
Not Least

I n the previous story, I wrote about Catherine, my adventurous first-born daughter who lives out of a suitcase. This entry is about my baby, Donna, and it bookends the collection nicely. Whereas Catherine is ready, shoot, aim in her approach to life, Donna's approach is more measured and thoughtful. I think that's because she spent most of her life observing her older brothers and sisters, learning from their mistakes and building on their successes.

It's hard to imagine it now, but Donna was the shy one in our family. As a child, she never wanted to leave the house or my side. Coaxing her to attend school often led to heartbreaking and tearful mornings: my heart, her tears. And when company came to visit, she often hid in the closet. I suppose it didn't help that her father was always joking about selling her off. But that was his sense of humor for you. If he wasn't trying to sell one of his kids, he was trying to marry them off.

I often wonder how she went from being my little shadow to the leading lady in all our lives. Apart from the milestones that we celebrated, i.e., her birthdays, first communion, prom, and graduations she remained under the radar. A quick survey of my children didn't reveal much in the way of mischief. Although they did direct me to her high school and college friends. But I suspect they're sworn to silence. And perhaps it's better that I don't know.

What I do know is that when anyone needs advice or a clear-headed assessment of their situation be it personal or professional, Donna is our go to girl. All her siblings and her friends turn to her,

the wise youngest sister. My husband would say it's because she paid her dues. Whether she was making sandwiches for Jimmy, serving as a clothes rack while shopping with Catherine, or explaining credit card return policies to Beth ("No Beth, you can't return the jeans in exchange for cash"). Donna is the hub around which we all revolve.

𝒮𝓃

Living Your Best Life

By my son, Jimmy

To say that I was close to my parents and grandmother is an understatement. For my entire life, I either lived with them or within a mile of them. (My grandmother lived with my parents most of her life.)

My wife Anna and I raised our two sons with the intention of gifting them with the same closeness and love. And our boys were fortunate enough to have two sets of grandparents with whom they were very close and saw often.

My grandmother died in 1989 and my dad in 2015. My beloved mom, passed away on December 22, 2020 from complications due to Covid-19. But she didn't die alone. We, her children, were blest to be with her and send her off with stories, music, laughter, and love. It's just what she wanted.

Strange as it may sound, her passing has not left a hole in our hearts. I suspect that's because our hearts are so full of love, and our heads so full of memories, that death is only a question of geography. And, geographically speaking, we know exactly where we are on the maps of lives. Our parents made sure to give us our bearings at a young age. So, while there is loss, we are not lost.

That doesn't make me any less sad for their passing. My dad, being the quintessential Irishman that he was, took a pragmatic approach to life and death. He used to jocularly refer to the obituaries as the 'Irish Sports Pages.' He was an inveterate wake-goer like his father before him. As are we, his children. For him it was important that one of us show up and represent the family.

Lately it occurs to me that as we get older, wakes become the counterpoints to weddings. For my dad, funerals represented the life-affirming traditions of remembrance and continuity in honor of the deceased. They are meditations on how to be your best self in the time that remains. He made this clear to me one day when I was 17 and we were attending the wake of a young man who had died before his time.

While my dad related to my sisters as if he were handling fine bone china, he took a man-to-man approach with his boys. Being a sensitive and sentimental man — qualities he kept hidden for fear of revealing his true feelings — he dealt with life's challenges with realism and humor, sometimes arriving directly to the point before we were ready. And so, that day he asked me point blank. "Why are you so sad?"

And I responded that I was sad not only because death had cut short a young life but because, surely, it must have left the parents bereft as only the loss of a child can do. To which he responded, "Jimmy, everyone gets their time in the box. You can't do anything about that. But what you can do something about, is the time God gives you while you're outside the box."

He went on to explain how people often chase things that may not have added as much meaning to their lives as they had thought. Or, worse, they neglected the things that were important. I didn't understand it much at the time, but as I got older, I came to appreciate his wise words more and more.

And, because the universe tends to work in symmetry, not long after that conversation I had with my dad, my grandmother shared some of out-of-the-box thinking she had about life.

My grandmother was a very beautiful woman, widowed at a young age. During one brief point in her life, she lived in a residence built by the parish church in our neighborhood. She had many friends and just as many admirers. There was one man who fancied her. And when I asked her about whether she had considered some companionship in the winter of her life, she brushed it off like snowflakes on a sleeve.

This man wasn't the man for her she said. And when I asked her why, she said because he was "afraid of death," which seemed like a natural thing to me at the time. Who wouldn't be afraid of death, I thought? When I asked her why it would be a bad thing to be afraid of death, she replied, "If he's afraid of dying, then he's also afraid of living. And that's no way to spend your life, afraid of what might happen if..."

As she looked beyond me into a more distant future, or perhaps it was the past, she also provided this word of caution. "Death is the point where your past catches up to your future, where you stand in judgement before God." And she concluded, "It's not how you die but how you live that counts."

They taught me a valuable lesson; every moment of every day is an opportunity to live your best life.

Back in Time

By the time you get to this final story, you would have read a great deal about the July Festival fundraiser in support of Our Lady of Mount Carmel Church and School. I have been a regular at the "Feast" ever since they began holding it on Herman Avenue in the '40s, before it moved to the schoolyard in the '50s.

That tradition was passed on to my children and it continues till this day. It's the best place to meet new friends, renew old friendships, and relive the memories of a lifetime.

As my husband, Jimmy, would often say, "You can take the girl out of the Neighborhood. But you can't take the Neighborhood out of the girl." And he was right.

One summer not too long ago, I was standing at the corner of Detroit Avenue and West 69th waiting for the procession to start when a familiar figure caught my eye. It was my friend Michael. He waved and crossed the street smiling as he came toward me. He gave me a big hug.

Michael and I had been friends ever since childhood. In a neighborhood that was predominately boys it was a challenge to find a best friend. Lucky for me, Michael became mine. We would sit on his steps for hours talking, laughing, and telling stories. He had my back, and I had his. He was like a brother but in low key kind of way. He never told me what to do, where to go, or how to behave.

Eventually we grew up and went our separate ways. We got married, raised our children, and retired to the suburbs but we always returned every summer to The Feast.

"Louisa, let's go back in time!" he said. I knew exactly what he had in mind. We began to walk down West 69th street, stopping in front of nearly every house. Every house had a story. And we'd always start by saying... "Do you remember?"

And we sure did remember. We started with Squeaky's house and recalled that he was always into something. We walked past Isabella's Bakery and smiled, remembering all the bread runs between Sunday Mass and dinner.

As we walked past Goose's old house it occurred to us that nearly everyone in the neighborhood had a nickname. My brothers Carmen and Tony were called Rhino and Lardy. My husband was just called "Irish" by the old timers who gave him permission to marry me.

We passed Michael's old house and my house too. And next to my house, was where my cousin, Wicky, lived. I could just see his car parked right in front of his door. What a crew we had! Little did I know that this walk down memory lane was to be our last one.

Let's face it, we're all getting older and forgetting things. And every year I have fewer and fewer friends with whom to share these memories. It would be a terrible waste and so I wanted to see them live on somehow. That's why I wrote this book.

I also wanted to pay tribute to my late husband, Jimmy, who will live on forever in my heart. As another Cleveland boy, Bob Hope, once so eloquently put it, "Thanks for the memory." I'd also like to thank all of you for joining me on my journey back in time and for sharing in some of those memories. I hope you enjoyed reading them as much as I did writing them

God bless you all!

(1939 – 2020)

About the Author

Louise Ricci Mulgrew grew up on the lower Westside of Cleveland in an Italian-American neighborhood. She was a tomboy, musician, marble champion and cosmetologist before she bucked tradition to marry her charming Irish-American husband, James (Jimmy) B. She married him on one condition — that they stay in "the neighborhood." He was as good as his word as they raised their seven children there.

The Times of Our Lives – Tales from an Italian Neighborhood *is a step back in time. It recounts the memories, the myths, and the moments of a close-knit group of family and friends. In addition to her stellar career as wife and mother, Louise has added a new skill to her growing list of accomplishments – storyteller.*

www.ingramcontent.com/pod-product-compliance
Lightning Source LLC
LaVergne TN
LVHW051307080426
835509LV00020B/3144